● Embrace the new sunrise in life: the dawn of possibility! ●

DEMOLISH YOUR OBSTACLES

TRANSFORM YOUR ADVERSITIES INTO MASSIVE SUCCESS

AF081049

SANTANU GHOSH

New Delhi • London

BLUEROSE PUBLISHERS
India | U.K.

Copyright © Santanu Ghosh 2024

All rights reserved by author. No part of this publication may be reproduced, stored in a retrieval system or transmitted in any form or by any means, electronic, mechanical, photocopying, recording or otherwise, without the prior permission of the author. Although every precaution has been taken to verify the accuracy of the information contained herein, the publisher assumes no responsibility for any errors or omissions. No liability is assumed for damages that may result from the use of information contained within.

BlueRose Publishers takes no responsibility for any damages, losses, or liabilities that may arise from the use or misuse of the information, products, or services provided in this publication.

For permissions requests or inquiries regarding this publication, please contact:

BLUEROSE PUBLISHERS
www.BlueRoseONE.com
info@bluerosepublishers.com
+91 8882 898 898
+4407342408967

ISBN: 978-93-6452-504-6

Cover design: Shivam
Typesetting: Namrata Saini

First Edition: August 2024

I dedicated my printed book to my father, who planted the seed of knowledge in my mind and nurtured it; To my mentor, Mr. Ved Prakas, who illuminated the path with wisdom through life's labyrinthine moments; to my wife, my unwavering pillar of support; and to my son, the beacon of light in my life.

Testimonial

I am absolutely delighted to share my thoughts on this transformative book by Santanu Ji, one of the most respected Mental Wellness Coach. As the Founder of Program Your Mind Organization, I have seen firsthand the remarkable power of mindset and proactive action in overcoming challenges and achieving success. This book captures these principles beautifully, offering you a comprehensive roadmap for personal growth and triumph.

In Chapter 1: Dispel Your Misconceptions, you will be encouraged to challenge common beliefs, embrace challenges, take responsibility, and find solutions even amidst adversity. The insights on overcoming mental barriers will provide you with a solid foundation for the journey ahead.

Chapter 2: The Power to Demolish Your Obstacles explores the shadows of despair, offering strategies to break free from the chains of negative thinking. This chapter is a powerful reminder that our greatest limitations often lie within our own minds.

Chapter 3: Mastering the Art of Harnessing Your Inner Power delves deep into the mind's potential. From understanding the relationship between the brain and mind to unlocking the power of mindset, this section is filled with wisdom. It will guide you in shifting from an unresourceful state of mind to a resourceful one and cultivating a growth mindset.

Chapter 4: Unshackling Consciousness addresses the mental 'viruses' that hinder our progress. You will find practical advice on creating a positive media diet, understanding the impact of your inner circle, and transforming your self-talk.

Finally, Chapter 5: Roadmap to Triumph lays out the final steps to success, offering a clear and strategic path to achieve extraordinary outcomes. The blueprint for strategic goal setting and the emphasis on assessing your present state are essential for anyone striving for success.

This book is not just a guide; it is a catalyst for change. It empowers you to break free from limitations, harness your inner power, and achieve your dreams. I highly recommend it to anyone committed to personal growth and success.

With best wishes for your journey,

VED

Founder, Program Your Mind Organization

About the Author

I am Santanu Ghosh, a Mental Wellness Coach, Subconscious Mastery Coach, Counselor, and Mentor, and the Founder Director of the 'Institute of Mental Wellness'. I am dedicated to serving individuals who face various challenges in life, helping them to achieve the life of their dreams.

With a profound understanding of the science of the mind, I have transformed my own life and assisted thousands of others in transforming theirs. With over 19 years of experience in the education and coaching sectors, including serving as a Director of an educational institution, I have passionately pursued the science of the mind since childhood, eventually mastering it through practical experience. This journey led me to realize my mission: to guide others in overcoming challenges and obstacles, enabling them to lead lives filled with success, happiness, and prosperity.

Having encountered significant challenges in my own life, I discovered how to easily overcome any obstacle and lead an exceptional life by awakening the infinite power within myself. As my mindset shifted, so did my circumstances. With the knowledge, tools, and techniques accumulated over the years, I can also help you overcome any struggles you face and steer you towards living your best life.

From initiating the transformation of your mindset to awakening the infinite potential of your mind, I can guide and support you at every step. Whether it's setting and achieving your goals, devising strategies, or overcoming obstacles that stand in your way, I am here to assist you. Together, we can propel you to the next level of recognition, success, health, wealth, love, relationships, and happiness, regardless of your current situation.

Acknowledgement

I would like to express my deepest gratitude to my family for their unwavering support throughout this journey. To my spouse, who endured late nights sleeps to support me with a smile, and to my son, who inspired me with his boundless sacrifices.

I would like to express my deepest gratitude to my father, [Mr. Mangala Prasad Ghosh, Retired assistant teacher], who took the responsibility of my entire family during my adversities, thank you for being my pillar of strength and my greatest champion and my elder sister (Swagata Maity) whose unwavering support and encouragement have been the cornerstone of my journey in writing this book. Your wisdom, patience, and constant motivation have inspired me to push beyond my limits and strive for excellence. I am profoundly grateful for the countless hours you dedicated to discussing ideas, reviewing drafts, and offering invaluable advice.

A special thanks to my Guru, Mr. Ved Prakash (Author & NLP Trainer), for believing me and helping to transform my life.

Heartfelt thanks to my friend Gopal Barman (Author, Setback to Comeback), whose constructive criticism and guide strengthened the narrative. My heartfelt thanks to my all friends especially to Subhajit Rout for giving me hand holding support.

I am really thankful to you Arpita, your love has been a profound teacher in my life's journey. The moments we shared together and the lessons learned from your departure have both been pivotal turning points. Your presence brought me growth, joy, and understanding, while your absence taught me resilience, introspection, and the strength to embrace change. Thank you for being a significant part of shaping my life.

This book would not be the same without the exceptional cover design by [designer's name] and the captivating illustrations by [illustrator's name]. Their creativity brought the book to life.

The editorial team at [publishing house] deserves applause for their insightful feedback and dedication to shaping this manuscript.

Finally, to the readers who embark on this adventure with me, thank you for giving these book a home in your heart.

Contents

Introduction 1

Chapter-1: Dispel Your Misconceptions 4
    Accepting Challenges over Problems: 10
    Taking Responsibility and Acting Proactively: 10
    Overcoming Mental Barriers: 11
    Finding Solutions amidst Adversity: 11

Chapter-2: The Power to Demolish Your Obstacles 12
    Shadows of Despair: 19

Chapter-3: (Part-I) Mastering the Art of Harnessing Your Inner Power 30
    Unveiling the Challenges: Understanding Why Most People Cannot Harness the Power of Their Minds 30
    The Enigmatic Relationship Between Brain And Mind 35
    Unlocking Potential: Exploring The Power Of Mindset 37
    The Influence of Mind-set on Internal Representation and State of Mind 40
    How to Shift Yourself from Unresourceful State Of Mind to Resourceful State Of Mind 45
    The Blueprint for a Growth Mindset 52
    The Journey Within: Exploring Self-Love as a Pathway to Discover Your True Self 55
    Believe is Power 64
    Transform Your Life: A Comprehensive Guide to Change Beliefs 68

Chapter-4: PART-2 Unshackling Consciousness: Liberating the Mind's Virus 72

    Creating a Positive Media Diet: Curating Content for Mental Health 80

    Understanding the Impact: Why Your Inner Circle Matters . 81

    Transforming Thoughts: How Self-Talk Shapes Your Reality 82

Chapter 5: Roadmap to Triumph: Unveiling the Steps to Success 86

    Defining Success: Understanding What It Truly Means 87

    Essential Give up: Key Steps to Achieve Extraordinary Success 96

    Strategic Goal Setting: Your Blueprint for Success 107

    Assessing Your Present State: A Vital Step towards Success 121

    Crafting the Path to Triumph: Strategic Planning for Success 122

    The Momentum of Action: Mastering the Push-Pull Method for Achieving Success 126

Introduction

First of all, I am writing this book not to share my life story, sorrows and pains with you. Throughout the book, you will find the secret to success by demolishing the obstacles of life that you are often facing in your life. This book is the perfect lighthouse of which indicates or directs how to overcome all the problems and adversities of your life and how to achieve massive success.

I am sure if you go through the book and follow the tools and techniques shared in it, it can bring an unexpected transformation to your life. There are such so many directions in this book which must show you the perfect way of success in any situation in life. Not only that you can find other real ways and get new inspiration to live the life of your dreams, you will also come to know how you can be happy and prosperous.

The main purpose of our lives is to become happy and prosperous, to improve life. I don't know what situation you are in when you are reading this book. Maybe you are moving towards the peak of improvement in your life, or you are drowning in the midst of adversity or problems, and you are running around with disorientation. But practically proven that if you implement all the tools and techniques mentioned in this book in your life, you can definitely take yourself to the next level in the fastest way. This book is going to be one of the 'game changers' in your life.

I am truly honored to be able to share these important life-transforming tools and techniques with you. And I am very confident that any chapter, tool or technique in this book will add great value to your life.

Every day at every moment some events are happening in our lives, some of the events or accidents destroy all the rhythms of our lives, take away the happiness of life, make life miserable and make us trapped in the net of problems. Like Abhimanyu of the Mahabharata, we all know how to enter Chakravyuh but do not know how to get out of that Chakravyuh. We can earn a vast amount of knowledge from our textbooks, we can learn a lot from different books, but they merely teach us how to implement those knowledges in our daily practical lives, as a result, whenever we face obstacles in real life, we get disoriented. Education surely helps us gain knowledge, but we need to understand the difference between real-life and mythic knowledge. Our conventional education system often overlooks the profound impact and workings of the 'Mind' and 'thought'. It fails to educate us on how deeply these faculties influence and guide us, leaving unexplored the intricate dynamics of our 'Mind' and 'Thought' processes. How does it work and what is its effect? We can never learn these from our conventional education system. Our traditional education system doesn't teach you why or how to control your emotions or how your behavior changes with time and situation. The opposite of 'sorrow' is 'happiness' - we must know it from our textbooks, we can also know what the meaning of happiness or sadness is! But please tell me what the word 'happiness' means to you (i.e.,, feeling) can it mean the same to me! You may be 'happy' if you spare time with your family; I am 'happy' when I get love and affection, and others can be happy if he/she earns a lot of money. Just like that, the meaning of 'success' varies from person to person! The meaning of love, happiness and prosperity differs for each person. The dreams of life and even the meaning of life also varied from person to person! Naturally, everyone's obstacles and malignancies in life are different, but the purpose of each of us is to overcome the obstacles of life and devote ourselves to the pinnacle of success, to live a happy, prosperous and meaningful life. The first step in achieving this objective is to find the root cause of the problems.

The second step is to search for power or resources to demolish them. The third step is to overcome all the adversities by increasing and consolidating strength and resources, only then we reach the last step, i.e., the MASSIVE SUCCESS. I promise this book will help you think and respond differently, and help you to get positive results in each and every area of life i.e., health, wealth, success, love and relationships and happiness. Not only that, but this book will make you ready to overcome all the obstacles by developing your mental strength unprecedentedly.

Follow each of the tools and techniques in this book with determination and faith to get what you desire for the lifestyle of your dreams, and you will surely find success.

CHAPTER-1

Dispel Your Misconceptions

When faced with problems in life, when adversity becomes a part of life, people often feel disoriented and helpless. One problem can lead to another, creating a black cloud of uncertainty in the mind. Over time, this can lead to mental and physical exhaustion, impairing one's ability to think clearly and make sound judgments. Internal conflicts and mental turmoil further diminish the capacity to take decisive action and make informed decisions.

In this very moment when you are going through this book, I can admit that you are now under one or more problems, and if so, I am sure that you are busy trying to find out the way to come out of that situation and are probably trying your best to come out of it. So let me discuss some important issues in this chapter so that you can come out of many misconceptions about life's problems or adversities first.

Firstly, you will have to remember that you are not the only person in this world who is in problems. It's important to recognize that everyone faces different problems in life. These problems add variety and depth to our existence, much like different colors that make life vibrant and interesting. Without these problems, life could become monotonous, akin to losing interest in a favorite food if it were served every day.

Secondly, many individuals, like you, encounter numerous challenges in life, yet many have successfully overcome them. So, what is the essence of this? Any problem or adversity can be conquered; therefore, never perceive difficulties as insurmountable. Reflect on your past experiences where you triumphed over adversities that once seemed daunting. Remember when you struggled with math in fifth grade! Or when you competed in school sports, facing opponents head-on! Today, you stand here having surmounted countless hardships.

If you examine these instances closely, you'll realize that in every scenario, you prevailed because you approached them as 'challenges' rather than 'problems'. Here lies my first piece of advice: from this moment onwards, view whatever difficulties you face not as 'problems' but as 'challenges'. This shift is crucial because it plays a significant psychological role; our minds naturally recoil from the word 'problem', but embracing 'challenges' empowers us to confront them directly.

By embracing this mind-set shift, you'll witness a remarkable transformation in how you perceive and handle challenges. The fear associated with problems will diminish, replaced by a proactive approach fuelled by the belief that every challenge is an opportunity for growth.

Secondly, whatever you're experiencing in life is never permanent; change is inevitable with time. However, waiting passively for circumstances to improve could take years or even ages without guaranteeing desired results. Conversely, taking proactive steps and assuming responsibility can swiftly transform adversity into tremendous success.

Let us share with you a moral story so that you can understand how taking action can transform an unfavorable, hostile and mal environment into a favorable one.

Two friends, Suba and Shinu, lived in a remote village in West Bengal, India, friends of the same heart. They are so close as if they are two yolks on the same stalk; they played together, studied at the same school and grew up together since childhood. Even though they are adults, their friendship is as before. Both of them love their small village and the villagers' best, the environment of the village, the river from which the village women fetch water for cooking and drinking, the pond where two friends bathe together, the trees and paths are very dear to them. The two friends also became very popular with the villagers for their friendly and benevolent nature. All in all, their lives were very enjoyable.

Suddenly there was a drought in that village due to the scarcity of rain. Slowly the pond in which they bathed dried up, and the river water they drank and used for cooking also dried up slowly. The whole village cries out for water, and the two friends are stirred in their hearts - how will they survive in such an adverse situation and what will happen to the villagers! The two started discussing together; Suba said something must be done so that they themselves, their families, and the villagers can all be safe and secure. Shinu says, "What can we do in this situation? What else do we have in our hands except waiting for the rain to fall in this extremely cruel game of nature! Besides, the best way is for us to move with our families to a place where there is enough water so that we and our families can survive."

Suba listens with all his heart and returns home without any answer. All night, he thought, what can be done? His friend's advice is not bad; they can leave the village and go somewhere else with their family to survive. But his mind refuses to accept in any way, the village where he grew up from childhood, the village from which he got so much love and success, how can he run away with his family thinking of his own interests when the village and the villagers are facing danger! No! It can never be! During the night, Suba kept thinking about what else could be done. In the morning he woke up and went to the river bed and took the basket and spade with him. Excavation begins, after digging quite a bit on the first day; he returns home by exhausted and finds Shinu sitting there. Shinu happily breaks the good news that he had found a house in town for rent and he can also find for Suba if he wants to. Both of them are tired so they don't talk much, everyone goes home. Early in the morning, Suba went as usual to the place where he was digging in search of water and started digging. In this way, after digging the ground every day, at the end of the fifth day, he finds water under the ground, that is, ultimately, he digs a whole well, and shouting 'I did...I did' with joy. Hearing his screams the villagers ran to the place, and were surprised and burst with joy. The problem was solved, his friend Shinu also returned home from the city after hearing the good news. The villagers, including Shinu, are all proud of Suba and applaud him. They blessed Suba from the core of their heart

MORAL: *No matter how unfavorable the situation is, if you take responsibility without waiting for time, it can definitely be changed.*

'Like shadows in sunlight, problems persist until we confront them. Running only casts them farther ahead, but facing them allows the light of solutions to shine through.'
-Santanu Ghosh

I'm sure you don't want to be 'Shinu' who wanted to wait for the time to solve the problem, wanted to run away from it. You must want to be another 'Suba' who did not wait for the situation to change with time, did not run away from the fear of problems, took responsibility on his own shoulders to make the adverse situation favorable and succeeded in not only saving himself or his family but also saving the lives of the entire village.

Thirdly, remember that every problem has a solution. There is no problem in this world that cannot be solved. You may feel that you are trying hard to find a solution in different ways, so why can't you find the solution? I am saying without belittling your efforts, efforts turn into success only when you can get out of the mental block, i.e.,, no matter how hard you work, if your mind is stuck in the problem, and then it is never possible to get the solution you want, just like drowning in water we cannot breathe. No matter how many problems you are facing, if you can overcome the obstacles mentally, you can get out of there quickly. Actually, the problem is like a spherical puzzle, it is difficult to find a solution from within. But when problems are going on in your life, you are definitely drowning in them! Then where is your light house?

The international border, the wall of China can stop the human body but not the mind, so overleap and cross the mental barrier; it will become easier to overcome the obstacles. There is another story that can inspire you to gain tricks of crossing mental barrier-

A 12 to 13-year-old boy is very excited to see Pole-vault in the Olympics and insists to his parents that he will learn the sport, and proposed his parents to allow him to learn this sport and requested to appoint a coach for proper training. His parents agreed and sent him to a pole-vault training centre for proper coaching. The coach also agreed to coach him after seeing his enthusiasm. His training continued every day, but the boy could not reach any more. Days passed but the boy could not imagine how it is possible to jump so high with the help of a narrow, long stick and cross the bar. He was becoming fated and hopeless. The coach could not bring him under control in any way despite showing and explaining in many ways. Finally, the coach called him one day and told him that first you take your mind across the scale; your body will follow your mind. The boy really, really sees in his mind that he has crossed the threshold, and when he comes to practice the next day, he can actually pole-vault successfully.

Moral: *Beyond the boundaries of our mental limitations lies the terrain of possibility. To conquer our problems and reach our destination, we must boldly cross that line, for therein lies the path to great achievement.*

Unexpected problems in life are like storms, which test the strength of our intellectual power to resolve them and the depth of our wisdom. Just as a sailor relies on a compass to navigate a rough boisterous ocean, so are we, who rely on a map of our values and experiences to chart a course through the challenges that surround us.

In the face of great adversity, our thoughts are like sails that carry us forward, catching the wind of hope and determination. And when the storm is over, we not only emerge unscathed but retained with new strength, a new clarity of purpose and a deeper understanding of ourselves.

> *'Sometimes, the hurdles we face are the sparks that ignite our creativity, pushing us to innovate and think beyond the ordinary.'*

Important summary of the first chapter:

1. Say 'Challenges' not 'Problems' because our mind wants to run away from fear when we hear the word 'Problems' but we accept 'Challenges'. On the contrary challenges give us mental power to deal with it.

2. Any adversity can only be destroyed and turned into favor by facing it head on with responsibility and not running away from it.
3. There must be a solution to every problem, to get that solution you have to overcome mental barriers

Conclusion

In the journey through life, we often encounter challenges that can feel overwhelming and insurmountable. The first chapter of this book, "Dispelling Your Misconceptions," sheds light on essential truths about adversity and how we can navigate through it with resilience and determination.

Accepting Challenges over Problems:

One of the fundamental lessons from this chapter is the power of perception. By reframing our mind-set from viewing difficulties as "problems" to embracing them as "challenges," we empower ourselves mentally. This subtle shift allows us to approach adversity with a proactive attitude rather than succumbing to fear and avoidance. It reminds us that challenges are opportunities for growth and transformation, not merely obstacles to be feared.

Taking Responsibility and Acting Proactively:

The story of Suba and Shinu illustrates the profound impact of taking responsibility and proactive action in the face of adversity. While Shinu contemplated leaving their village to seek water elsewhere, Suba chose to take matters into his own hands. Through perseverance and determination, Suba not only found a solution but also became a source of inspiration and hope for his entire community. This narrative underscores the importance of confronting challenges head-on and assuming responsibility for shaping our destinies.

Overcoming Mental Barriers:

Another critical insight from the chapter emphasizes the role of our mental state in navigating challenges. Just as the young boy in the pole-vaulting story had to overcome his mental limitations before achieving physical success, we too must transcend our mental barriers to find solutions. By cultivating a mind-set of resilience, creativity, and openness, we enhance our capacity to overcome even the most daunting obstacles.

Finding Solutions amidst Adversity:

Lastly, the chapter highlights the belief that every problem carries within it the seed of a solution. It challenges us to look beyond immediate difficulties and tap into our inner resources—be it determination, creativity, or empathy—to find innovative solutions. Like a sailor navigating stormy seas, we rely on our values and experiences as guiding stars to chart a course through adversity, emerging stronger and wiser on the other side.

In conclusion, "Dispelling Your Misconceptions" invites us to embrace challenges as opportunities for growth, to take proactive steps towards solutions, and to overcome mental barriers that hinder our progress. By internalizing these principles, we equip ourselves with the resilience and clarity needed to navigate life's inevitable challenges with grace and fortitude.

As you embark on the chapters ahead, remember that each chapter builds upon these foundational insights, offering further guidance and wisdom to empower you on your journey of personal growth and transformation.

CHAPTER-2

The Power to Demolish Your Obstacles

'Hurdles fade when minds transcend, where belief and action blend, break the mental chains that bind, and leave your doubts behind.'

Before entering into the main subject of this chapter i.e.,, 'Finding Power', I would like to ask you which of the following is or are the biggest problems in your life right now, from which you want to get rid of quickly? Below is a list of some of the problems by which generally most of the people are stricken with, select your problems from among them, or if you have any other problem/s beyond that, then write it down carefully in this book. Only then when you reach the end of this book through by continuous applying the tools and techniques in this book, you will realize the true magical effects of this book.

PROBLEMS	MARK YOUR PROBLEM
Financial Instability: Income inequality, job insecurity, and rising living costs.	
Physical Health Concerns: Chronic illnesses, lifestyle diseases, and access to healthcare.	
Love and Relationships: Difficulty in finding and maintaining meaningful relationships.	
Personal Identity: Self-esteem issues, identity crises, and personal growth challenges.	
Family Issues: Conflict within families, parenting challenges, and generational gaps.	
Not getting success what you want	
Failing repeatedly	
Mental Health Challenges: Increasing rates of anxiety, depression, and stress.	
Debt and Financial Management: Credit card debt, student loans, and financial planning.	
Work-Life Balance: Challenges in balancing career demands with personal well-being.	
Social Isolation: Loneliness, lack of	

social support, and disconnected communities. Lack of meaningful connections and community support.	
Addiction and Bad Habits: Substance abuse, technology addiction, and unhealthy lifestyle choices.	
Career Dissatisfaction: Job dissatisfaction, work-life balance issues, and career transitions.	
Physical disability	

If there is anything else, mention it here...

I promise you again, you will not be the same person as you are now, and after completing this book, there will be huge positive changes in your life! So keep a good record of the current situation so that you can see what drastic changes have happened to you.

I know that after looking at all the problems, you may also think that all of those problems are going on in your life or most of the problems are going on in your life. However, if you look carefully at each problem, you will understand that if you want to get rid of them or eliminate them, it is not possible to solve them in the state in which all the problems have been created. Only more power or resources can demolish them. For example to get rid of financial problems, you need to become financially strong. In the case of impediments to love or family marital problems then you need resources like love, happiness and peace to solve them. To overcome all such adversities, we either need more power or resources. You will be able to overcome the obstacles only when your strength or resources are greater than the obstacles. If not for the pressure of adversities, the stress of an unfavorable condition will smashed you at a glance. Before sharing a great moral story about this, I want to ask some questions that have arisen in my mind and I want you to ask these questions to yourself.

You are having financial problems, you are in debt, tell me who would like to help you with money in that situation? If you are very lucky, you might get help from someone else, but at the same time, won't the insults you have to digest from that person hurt you more? Won't it give you pain like a septic sore or give you trouble after trouble? Once deprived of love by a lover, can it ever be possible to get back love from the lover by begging for love, shedding tears, pleading, even being most obedient to? Or, will someone else immediately come to you and offer you love by saying, "No matter, don't worry; I am here for you, since now I will love you"?

What I mean to say is that there are solutions to the problem, there are enough power and resources to destroy adversity, but if you seek it from the wrong place or person, if you adopt the wrong approach, it will increase the danger, not reduce it, you will get into the deeper holes of problems. In other words, to face any challenge, proper energy or resources are required along with its proper application and proper approach.

Let's now share the moral story:-

Once upon a time, in a small village nestled between towering mountains and dense forests, lived a young woman named Maya. Maya was known for her vibrant spirit and unwavering optimism. She had a dream of becoming a renowned potter, crafting beautiful pieces that would bring joy to people's lives.

One fateful day, a severe storm swept through the village. The torrential rains and powerful winds wreaked havoc, destroying homes and livelihoods. Maya's pottery studio, her cherished sanctuary, was not spared. The storm shattered her carefully crafted pieces, leaving behind a scene of utter devastation.

Maya was heartbroken. She stood amidst the ruins of her dreams, feeling as empty and twisted as an old, discarded bottle. The villagers, who had always admired her work, tried to console her, but nothing seemed to lift her spirits. She felt as though the storm had not only destroyed her studio but also her very soul.

Days turned into weeks, and Maya struggled to find the strength to rebuild. She wandered the village, lost in thought, until one day she stumbled upon an old potter named Arjun. Arjun was known for his wisdom and skill, and he had faced many adversities in his life.

Seeing Maya's forlorn expression, Arjun invited her to his workshop. It was a humble place, filled with pots of various shapes and sizes, each telling a story of resilience and perseverance. Arjun handed Maya a piece of clay and asked her to mould it.

With hesitant hands, Maya began to shape the clay. As she worked, Arjun shared his own story. He spoke of times when he felt broken, twisted by life's hardships, much like the clay in Maya's hands. But through those adversities, he had learned to reshape himself, finding strength and beauty in the process.

"Adversity," Arjun said, "is like a force that can twist and bend us, much like this clay. But it's in those moments of being twisted that we discover our true form, our resilience, and our ability to transform."

Inspired by Arjun's words, Maya poured her heart into her work. She realized that just as the storm had twisted her life; it had also given her the opportunity to rebuild herself anew. She began to see the broken pieces of her old life not as remnants of failure, but as materials for a stronger, more resilient future.

Over time, Maya's studio was reborn. Her new creations reflected the depth of her experiences, each piece a testament to her journey through adversity. The villagers marvelled at her work, not just for its beauty, but for the powerful story it told.

Maya's pottery became renowned far beyond her village, inspiring others to see their own adversities as opportunities for growth. She learned that while adversities can twist and bend us like an empty bottle, it is within our power to reshape ourselves into something stronger and more beautiful.

Moral: *And so, Maya's story became a beacon of hope, reminding everyone that within every adversity has the potential to transform and birth something extraordinary.*

'Only through pure belief can we alchemize our adversities into the gold of massive success.'

But here is a big question: From where can we get this power or resources whatever you call it? Or is there any superstitious power really something by which one can destroy all obstacles in life and move forward?

The answer is 'Yes, of course!'

In a bustling city, there was a young man named Alex who faced constant challenges in his life. He struggled with self-doubt and adversity, unsure of how to overcome the hurdles that seemed to block his path at every turn. He failed to continue his business due to financial problem, was facing pressure from money lender. Besides his wife left him and went away with another young taking her baby. As if he was sinking and drowning in the ocean of problems.

One day, Being hopeless and feeling overwhelmed by his problems, Alex sought the help of a wise old sage who was known for his profound wisdom and insight. Alex poured out his heart, explaining all the difficulties he faced and asking for guidance on how to overcome them.

The sage listened intently, nodding sagely as Alex spoke. When Alex finished, the sage looked at him kindly and said, "My dear boy, the power and resources to overcome your challenges lies within you. No one else can do it for you."

Alex was taken aback. He had expected the sage to offer him solutions or advice and he hoped for an amulet or stone from the sage so that he can overcome the adverse situation, but instead, he was told to look within himself. Feeling confused but intrigued, Alex asked, "But how? How can I find this power within me?"

The sage smiled knowingly and replied, "Through self-awareness and self-belief. You must first realize that you possess the strength and courage to face any challenge that comes your way. Once you believe in yourself, you will find that the obstacles you once thought insurmountable are merely stepping stones on your path to success."

With these words, the sage bid Alex farewell, leaving him to ponder his words. Over time, Alex began to see his challenges in a new light. Instead of feeling defeated, he started to view them as opportunities for growth and learning.

With each obstacle he overcame, Alex felt the power within him grow stronger. He no longer sought external help or validation, knowing that the key to his success lay within himself.

Years passed, and Alex became a successful businessman, known for his resilience and determination. When asked about his secret to success, he would simply smile and say, "The power to overcome adversity lies within each of us. We just have to believe in ourselves and never give up."

And so, the moral of the story is this: No matter how challenging life may seem, always remember that you have to have the power and resources within you to destroy any obstacle. You just have to believe and trust in yourself to realize that power and apply it properly.

After listening to the complete story, the question must be arising in your mind, if all the power lies within each of us, then why are almost 95% of the people suffering from various problems in life? Why do they get tired of struggling with life's obstacles? Or it is merely a story! Let me try to make you understand through my biography as well as the life stories of the world's greatest personalities what is the latent power that resides within us, which most people don't realize, but that power can bring us to the top of our success by destroying all obstacles?

Like Alex, I've had challenges in my life at different times, sometimes not just one problem - a series of problems at once that would be enough to make any person cringe. I have come back from the door of certain death (when I was injected wrongly and maybe the doctor didn't have anything to do), I lost my beloved 'Mother' for ever in my boyhood in the absence of me so I could not see her last breath, my studies were about to end (for doing terrible results in a class), I have seen my business worth lakhs of rupees turn into dust in the blink of an eye, and years after years I have endured demands, threats, insults from creditors, hiding in fear. At one point I went door to door to get a job to feed the child and families but all my trails were in vain. Once, I had to borrow the shoes to put on from other as I had no money to buy new shoes. In the most difficult situation of life, I have seen the dearly beloved person go away cruelly with another person. Honestly speaking, the cry of my empty heart didn't reach anyone's ears, neither any person, nor God heard it. So I am speaking from deep experience, no one will be with you in difficult situations or if there is someone, he will never try to understand your situation, instead he will think of you as his burden.

Shadows of Despair:

The financial strain was relentless, the bills piled up day by day and the stress grew daily. The savings that once provided a safety net have been wiped out. Phone calls from creditors became a daily torment; each ring was the sign of my failure. I sent countless job applications, hoping for a lifeline, but rejection letters became a familiar sight. Even though I got a job after looking for, I was a victim of politics before joining there and that too was cancelled. It seemed to me as if the world had closed to me and I had been seized in a puzzle with no way out, so committing suicide was the only way out.

Another devastating incident blew into my personal life and hurt me during a financial crisis. The one I loved, the one I believed from the core of my heart and I thought always she would be by my side, in happiness and sorrow, in good and bad times, through well and woe. But...but she also decided to leave me too. The words she told me still haunt me "I'm not with you anymore..." Her departure stabbed me in my heart.

Loneliness became my constant companion, sometimes it felt as if the walls of my room were squeezing me, suffocating me with their oppressive presence. Nights were the worst and most pathetic. When everyone fell asleep, I would lie awake at night and count the moments to pass. The restlessness and repentation swallowed me. Memories of sweet days played on my mind like a cruel joke, mocking the reality I was facing.

I used to question myself about my choices, my abilities, and my competence. The future seemed bleak, a void where there had once been hope. I felt abandoned by the world, with no one to comfort and nothing to comfort. Every day was a battle to continue, to find a reason to wake up in the morning and go to sleep at night. Depression clawed at my soul, threatening to pull me down under the earth.

In the depths of this pain I learned the harsh reality of life's unpredictability. Financial challenges, sinking my business, rejection and heartbroken situation all painted a picture of despair. Yet in the midst of these thousand obstacles, in the darkest moments, a small glimmer of the will to turn around began to shine in me. I realized that in the face of overwhelming odds I had only one choice to 'give in to despair or fight for hope.'

This chapter of my life was marked by deep pain, a time when everything seemed to fall apart. But it was actually a time of introspection. From there I began to understand the depth of my own power. The road ahead was uncertain and the wounds were deep but there was a glimmer of hope. I held onto the belief that a new chapter could emerge from the ashes of despair—a chapter of self-discovery, renewal, and ultimately redemption.

Relying on the light of that gentle hope, I sat down with a notebook and pen to write, with only one purpose, as a last effort, if at least I can discover myself! A pivotal moment in my solitude came when I decided 'enough is enough, now I have to take action, no matter how small!' One evening as the sun sank below the horizon, casting long shadows across my dimly lit room, I found myself at a cross road. The silence was deafening yet whispering a possibility, I sat down at my rickety wooden desk with a determination I hadn't felt in months, a notebook and pen, very simple tools in front of me that I hoped at least it will lift me out of the shadow of despair.

The first stroke of the pen felt awkward, almost unrecognizable, as if my hand had forgotten how to write under the weight of anxiety and doubt. But slowly the words of my heart began to flow on paper. I started making a list of the strengths or resources I needed in my current situation in raw and unvarnished honesty: money, wealth, job or business, enthusiasm, knowledge, skill, love, confidence, physical and mental well-being, cooperation, etc....

The list got quite long and when it was finished I started analyzing them. Looking at the list I realized that it was much more than just a collection of some powerful words. I sat down to analyze one by one word at a time, which of these long lists is the most urgent and important for me at the moment. After a hair-raising trial, I saw that the only 'money' that could be searched for would solve all my problems in an instant. At that time, the effects of **Coronavirus** have started around the world, the lockdown is going on all over the country, despite that, I tried a lot to get some small job, but at that time millions of people were unemployed, so that effort failed. I thought I would start a business, so I borrowed some money from my acquaintances, especially those who had benefited me in one way or another in my golden days. The experience became bitterer, as if everyone thought I was untouchable, when they saw me, they turned their faces and disappeared with the speed of an arrow. Even though it hurt me, I realized that "don't help the drowning people, there is a high possibility of your own death" - this thought is running in everyone's mind. Though I was very much grieved I consoled myself 'there should not be any grief to a penny less man'.

Necessarily again I sat down with that simple tool but invaluable resource i.e., pen and paper to analyze. And I discovered one thing, really shockingly, that I had no direct control over anything except for one or two of the things I had made a list of. I began to analyze better, -When the first big challenge came in my life, my 'mother' died at a young age, within 15 days my high school results was published and I failed, my first love left almost at the same time. I also was analizing carefully, what exactly I did then! How did I come out of that situation in an immature state! This second day of analysis is the brightest, most successful and happiest day of my life in the face of real adversity because I discovered that priceless resources, the infinite power that no one else can give and also no one can take away, that power, that resources is only mine. I found that strength i.e., 'mental strength', the power of mind, got that 'mental resource' - patience, faith, resilience, confidence. I know the journey ahead was still unget-at-able, but it didn't seem arduous anymore.

'The light of hope can pierce the darkest clouds of despair, illuminating a path forward—stay hopeful, and see the world transform.'

I know that like most people, you may doubt 'MENTAL STRENGTH or MIND POWER'; you too can question your ability to influence reality and achieve significant changes! Skeptic thinking, disbelief, and vague ideas or ignorance about the mind can lead to questions that make it difficult for people to accept that mental processes profoundly affect outcomes in real-life. People actually believe in instant results though they do not believe in many visible things also. But I would say to understand its power you need to give yourself some logic, to clarify any questions that arise in mind. I refer to several famous great personalities in the world to satisfy you logically, and to pay attention to these is more important because when a man is in a problematic situation, he thinks that such a problem has never existed in anyone's life, or arose before in anyone's life. Also, many people mistakenly believe that successful people were born with all the resources necessary for their success and never faced significant challenges. In reality, successful people have faced numerous obstacles and setbacks on their journey. Their life stories often include moments of setbacks and adversity that they overcome with strong determination and mental strength. Obstacles are present in every human life and will remain so, so it is necessary to observe well what extremely successful personalities do or what they have in them that makes them completely different from ordinary people. They certainly do not have any secret spells or magic wands! So, what is there? Let's unravel that mystery-

The first name I'll take is Oscar-winning actress Halle Berry, who was so poor, and financially challenged that she was sleeping in a homeless shelter at one point. Halle Berry had a reported net worth of $90 million at one point. Like Halle Berry there are thousands of such examples who could not be suppressed by economic problems. Howard Schultz, former CEO chairman of Starbucks, co-founders of Apple Computer Steve Jobs and Steve Wozniak, famous British businessman Richard Branson, India's youngest billionaire Nikhil Kamath, and many others belong to this category who come from extreme financial hardship or lower middle-class families but become one of the richest people in the world. These are a few examples of individuals who have come from poor or average financial backgrounds and have created massive success in their lives.

This is about financial problems. If you think that physical disability or feebleness is an obstacle in life that cannot be overcome and that you cannot achieve great success because the saying 'health is wealth' does not apply at all to this personality, how will wealth come without good health! No, my dear gentleman, it is absolutely wrong! Srikanth Bolla, a blind man from Hyderabad, India, was not even allowed to sit for the written competitive exams of IITs and NITs. Finally, he completed his degree from MIT, US, on scholarship. After returning from the United States in 2012, he established Bollant Industries Pvt. Ltd. It is a company where about 60 percent of the employees are from the poor background and physically challenged. There are also many examples whose names you may know: Jessica Cox, the world's first armless female pilot, Helen Keller, the famous deaf and dumb writer; Nobel Prize-winning scientist Albert Einstein, Stephen Hawking, the famous black hole theory inventor, Arunima Sinha, the first Indian woman who climbed to the top of Mount Everest with a prosthetic leg. And with all these famous people there are thousands more names on this list. Do you think all those people's journeys were thornless? No never! Their eternal secret of climbing on the peak of success, making their impassable way passable was nothing but Mind power, by which they overcame all obstacles in life.

People often misunderstand that when the environment becomes an obstacle, they cannot overcome it, and even their mental strength becomes useless. Yes, although it is true that we cannot always control our surroundings and environment, but we can control our reactions and approach by harnessing the power of our minds, transforming seemingly insurmountable obstacles into opportunities for growth and innovation. And as evidence in this regard, I would like to present the names of several great personalities.

Many have heard of Johnny Depp, in 2012, he set himself in the Guinness Book of World Records as the highest paid actor who spent his childhood as a nomad. He reportedly started smoking at age 12, started taking drugs at age 14, and dropped out of high school at age 16. Famous author Viktor Frankl, founder of logo therapy, Austrian psychiatrist, and Holocaust survivor, was sent to concentration camps in 1942. During his stay in various concentration camps, he lost his parents and wife in concentration camps within a few days. Try to think and imagine about the obstacles, mal environment and problems of that person who had to work hard, not having sufficient food, water to drink, room for shelter, and rest, rather, he was tortured cruelly, and in that very sequences he had lost his so many beloved person.

Dr. Sindhutai Sapkal, the lady called "Mother of Orphans", whose nickname was Chindhi, which means a torn piece of cloth, was born on 14th November 1948 (Died on 4th January, 2022), in Wardha, who was forced to drop out of fourth grade due to her family's commitment and early marriage. At the age of 10, she was married to a 30-year-old man. When she was twenty, her husband beat her and threw her away and she was then nine months pregnant. Later, on the same day, she gave birth to a baby girl in a barn and walked a few kilometres to her mother's house. Her mother drove her away without giving her shelter. In such a helpless situation, after finding nothing, she finally cut off her umbilical cord with a sharp stone. This incident left such a deep scar on her mind that she wanted to commit suicide. Later, she got rid of that thought and started begging at the railway station to bring after her daughter. While begging, she saw that there were many helpless children who were abandoned by their parents, and were begging with a lot of pain in their lives. She felt their pain and decided to adopt them. Her new war started, and she began begging loudly to put a handful of food in the mouths of the helpless children. Gradually, she decided she would adopt all the orphan kids there, and she did so. She had adopted and cared for more than fifteen hundred Orphan Children. Not only that, she had taken all responsibility for their education, marriage, and establishment. Many of them are now established as doctors, engineers, or lawyers. She had won over 700 awards and she spent all the prize money on her children. She was conferred the Padma Shri in 2021 in the Social Work category. Many of you may know the life story of Dr. Sindhutai Sapkal. This story is probably inspiring many of you, or will inspire many, but most do not know that her mind is the mastermind of this outstanding achievement. There was no one or nothing with her. With her, there was no society, no environment, and no relatives. Except only one resource, that is her '**mind**'. It was the mind that had shown her the way out of the most complex problems and given her the urge to live. She had many reasons to give up and commit suicide. Tell me what environment this woman received from childhood? How many problems has she faced in her life? Go inside and think deeply about her life. And if it is seen, there are countless people on this list too.

If we think that educational qualification or so-called brain is another big obstacle for us! Then I must say 'no'! There are thousands of names in this list; I have given only a few names as an example here, who have established themselves as one of the best despite this challenge in their lives.

Bill Gates or Mark Elliot Zuckerburg have established themselves as one of the richest people in the world, but both billionaires dropped out of college prematurely. The Wright brothers, the inventors of the flying machine, never had a secondary school education. Henry Ford's name is known to almost everyone, he also completed the eighth grade from a one-room school. If I say, mountains of names will be listed out, great people like Walt Disney, Kapil Dev, and Sachin Tendulkar are also in these categories.

Many of the great personalities I have named as examples have faced tough challenges in their lives that we can't even imagine and it's also good to know that they overcame not just one, but multiple challenges just because of their mind power. And the most joyful thing is that this is our very personal inner resource. You never have to look for this power or this resource in the outer world. It is only necessary to understand it and acquire the skills to use it in the right direction. In the next chapter of this book, I will share in detail various tools and techniques that can be used to realize and use this personal power to easily overcome any obstacles you may have.

Life is an uncertain and unpredictable journey full of challenges and obstacles. Although the obstacles may seem insurmountable at times, it is our 'mind' that holds the power to steer or sail our lifeboat in the right direction. A sailboat can move against the wind if its sails are properly adjusted. In the same way, if we can blow the wind in the sail of our mind with the help of the power of thought, incredible capacity for creativity, unshakable belief (in ourselves), perception, and decision-making skills, we can turn any adversity into an opportunity for growth and success if we can put the wind in the sails of the mind.

Remember *obstacles can never define our life but how we design our life to overcome it with the power of mind is our life.*

Reflection Paper (Individual Task)

- Reflect on a significant challenge or obstacle you have faced in your life. It could be related to finances, relationships, career, health, or any other area.

- Write a detailed reflection paper that includes the following:
  - **Introduction:** Describe the challenge you faced and its impact on your life.
  - **Analysis:** Apply the concept of "inner power" discussed in the chapter to analyze how you responded to the challenge. Discuss whether you recognized and utilized your inner resources effectively.
  - **Personal Growth:** Reflect on how the experience helped you grow as a person. Did it change your perspective on challenges? How did you emerge stronger from the situation?
  - **Lessons Learned:** Share any valuable lessons you gained from overcoming this challenge and how you intend to apply these lessons in future situations.
  - **Conclusion:** Summarize your reflections and insights gained from this exercise.

Conclusion:

In the exploration of "The Power to Demolish Your Obstacles," we have delved into the profound concept that obstacles in life are not insurmountable barriers but rather opportunities for transformation and growth. The journey through this chapter has been marked by introspection and the recognition that true power lies within each of us—the power of our minds.

Through compelling stories and reflective narratives, we have learned that adversity can twist and challenge us, much like clay in the hands of a potter. However, it is within these challenging moments that we discover our resilience and ability to reshape our lives. Maya's story of rebuilding her pottery studio after a devastating storm and Alex's journey from hopelessness to success illustrate this transformative process vividly.

The key takeaway from this chapter is clear: the power to overcome obstacles resides within us. It is not found in external circumstances or fleeting solutions but rather in our own mental strength, determination, and belief in ourselves. The sage's advice to Alex—that the solutions to his challenges lay within him—echoes throughout these narratives, reinforcing the notion that our internal resources are the most potent tools for navigating life's challenges.

The examples of individuals like Halle Berry, Srikanth Bolla, and Dr. Sindhutai Sapkal further underscore this principle. These remarkable individuals faced seemingly insurmountable odds—from homelessness and physical disabilities to personal tragedies—and yet, through the power of their minds, they not only persevered but also achieved extraordinary success and made profound contributions to society.

As we conclude this chapter, it is important to recognize that obstacles are not meant to defeat us but to strengthen us. They provide us with opportunities to harness our inner resources, develop resilience, and ultimately, transform our lives for the better. The path forward lies in understanding and cultivating our mental strength, embracing challenges as opportunities for growth, and believing steadfastly in our ability to overcome.

In the chapters ahead, we will explore practical tools and techniques to harness this inner power effectively, empowering you to navigate life's obstacles with confidence and achieve your fullest potential. Remember, the power to demolish your obstacles and transform adversity into success resides within you—it is yours to discover, cultivate, and unleash.

CHAPTER-3

(Part-I) Mastering the Art of Harnessing Your Inner Power

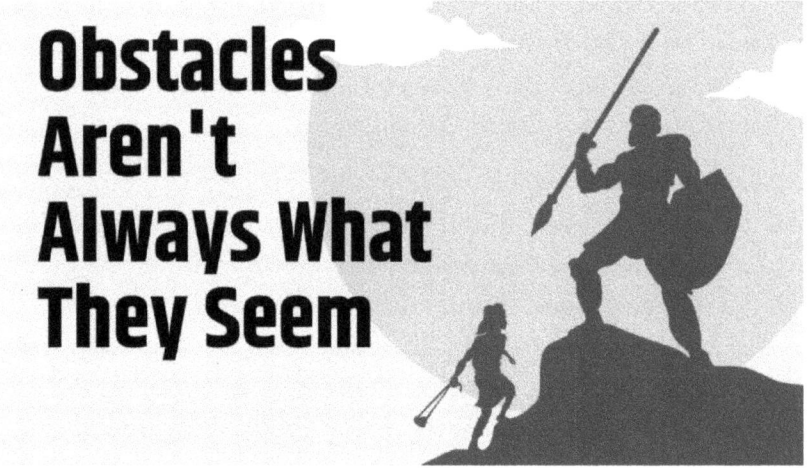

'Unleash the might of your mind; it holds the power to conquer any challenge life throws your way.'

Unveiling the Challenges: Understanding Why Most People Cannot Harness the Power of Their Minds

Hope you have no difficulty in understanding that within our minds lies an unlimited power that alone can save you in the most difficult times and situations, show you a new direction. Do think for a moment, and you will see some people succumb to small challenges and take extreme decisions like suicide, while many people decide to turn around even when faced with the most difficult obstacles in life. A man who has seen his house, family, home and even the last wealth burnt into ashes in front of his eyes, has managed to turn around and achieve another level of success in life because even though everything has been lost, he has not lost his hope and mental strength, did not give up.

But the question remains, 'Mind' is available to every person, so why can't every person use it properly for their betterment, to become happy? The real cause of it is most people don't want to master the art of using internal power because they don't want to take a little pain in the beginning to do so, they don't want to come out of their (What they consider to be their comfort and familiar zone, no matter how painful it is) comfortable and familiar zone. Most people believe that something will suddenly happen in a divine way or miraculously that will change everything in their lives. Psychology says people want to get everything without paying anything or without any effort. And that is why there is so much sadness, misery, pain of not getting, and despair in people's lives.

Let me share an interesting and wonderful story with you in this context, and then we shall learn about the tools and techniques of using inner power one by one.

In a small town nestled between rolling hills and whispering pines, there lived a young boy named Kovi. He was known for his skepticism towards anything he couldn't see or touch. Magic, mental strength and inner power were all mere fantasies to him, dismissed as tales spun by wishful thinkers. Instead, Kovi believed in hard work, tangible results, and the straightforward path to success. One sunny afternoon, as he kicked a soccer ball against the worn-out wall of the local gym, a coach named Mr. Thompson approached him. Mr. Thompson was renowned for his wisdom and unshakable belief in the power of the mind. He had observed Kovi for some time, noticing his talent but also his tendency to falter when faced with challenges. "Kovi," Mr. Thompson said, his voice carrying a hint of concern, "you have incredible potential, but I see you doubt the strength that lies within you."

Kovi shrugged, dribbling the ball absently. "I don't believe in all that mental stuff, coach. It's about skill and practice."

The coach smiled knowingly. "Skill and practice are crucial, but without mental strength, they can only take you so far. Let me show you."

Mr. Thompson took Kovi under his wing, teaching him some tools and techniques of mastering the art of harnessing inner power. Kovi, though skeptical at first, reluctantly agreed to try. He practiced visualizing scoring goals effortlessly, maintaining focus under pressure, and staying calm during intense matches.

Weeks passed, and Kovi diligently followed Mr. Thompson's guidance. Yet, despite his efforts, he didn't see any immediate improvement in his game. Doubt crept in once more, and Kovi grew frustrated.

"I'm doing everything you said, coach," Kovi admitted one day after practice. "But nothing's changing. Maybe this mental stuff just isn't for me."

Mr. Thompson nodded knowingly. "Kovi, true strength doesn't lie in seeing immediate results. It lies in persevering even when the path seems unclear."

With those words, Mr. Thompson devised a final test for Kovi. He set up a challenging obstacle course on the field, designed to push Kovi to his limits physically and mentally. As Kovi navigated through the course, doubts and fears surfaced, threatening to overwhelm him. But with each hurdle, he remembered Mr. Thompson's teachings – visualizing success, staying focused, and believing in his abilities.

At the end of the course, Kovi collapsed on the grass, exhausted yet exhilarated. He looked up to see Mr. Thompson smiling warmly at him.

"You did it, Kovi," the coach said. "You demolished every obstacle, not just with your physical strength, but with the power of your mind. That's the true essence of mental strength."

As Kovi caught his breath, a newfound understanding dawned upon him. It wasn't about instant success or visible outcomes. Mental strength was about the ability to overcome challenges, even when the odds seemed insurmountable.

From that day forward, Kovi approached every practice and game with a renewed sense of purpose. He continued to hone his skills, but now with the added confidence in his mental abilities. With each match, his performance improved, and his teammates noticed the change – not just in his game but in his demeanours.

As for Mr. Thompson, he watched proudly from the sidelines, knowing that he had not just taught a young boy about soccer, but about life's greatest lesson – the untapped power of the human mind. And within Kovi, he saw a future leader, guided not only by skill but by the inner strength that would carry him far beyond the soccer field.

Why are human beings different from other animals? - Because we have a powerful brain, surely you will agree! Now tell me, despite the fact that everyone has this upgraded and powerful brain, why is there so much difference from person to person? Why does a boy who has been declared an addled by his school and asked his mother not to send him to school discover something that lights up the world in the dark of night? The kid who somehow gets kicked out of his art college for lack of creativity becomes the best creative person in the world? 'Yes', there is a powerful tool behind those successes and that is our 'mind'. Creature has given each of us a powerful brain and to conduct the brain he has also installed software with it. And, this software in the form of mind which manages our powerful brain; this software actually makes so much difference from person to person. The better the software can be managed, the better the result in life is bound to be. In general, the mobile, laptop or computer that you use must have a hardware system and this hardware system is inactive until any software is installed on it. Again, no matter how powerful and upgraded version hardware is installed in your system, it will not work if the upgraded version software is not installed on it. Again, even with all the system updates, if you don't know or learn how to operate it, it's nothing more than a stupid box to you. And to operate it, whether you know anything about hardware or not, you must have knowledge about the software system, understand it well, then you can operate it properly. Through its use it will become possible to solve many complex problems easily; its creativity can also be used.

Now tell me we all have more or less an idea about the brain, but what percentages of people have an idea about the mind? Most people don't know about this powerful software or how to use it, so how to realize its infinite power and how to manage it? And if we can't manage it properly, it's almost impossible to manage the powerful brain that we have!

Try to understand another thing, you have both powerful upgraded version hardware and software systems but no antivirus installed in your software, and you connect your system to the Internet. Now tell me what happens? Within a few days, the virus will attack and collapse your system. Now take a good look and think about whether the same thing is happening in your life! You have a very powerful brain, a powerful 'mind' to manage it. But can you imagine how many viruses (negativity) are constantly entering from the environment you are in, the negative bombardment you are in, the content you are consuming throughout the day (from social media, television channels, newspapers, etc.), and how they are all affecting your mind and thought process! Research indicates that the fear of this virus has claimed more lives than the actual fatalities caused by the coronavirus worldwide. But why? - Because that virus had a greater impact on the mind in the form of fear than the physical effect. In the same way, the virus that enters your mind constantly, every day, is slowly making your life hellish.

So what? If you want to realize your mind power and use it for positive, constructive work and to get rid of your life challenges, you need to know about this powerful software. Let us go ahead, step by step:-

At first, we shall know about the 'MIND' as far as possible:-

The Enigmatic Relationship Between Brain And Mind

The relationship between brain and mind remains one of the most intriguing and mysterious in the vast landscape of human understanding. In the complex dance of human existence, the mind is the choreographer and the brain is the faithful and loyal performer. While the brain is the physical organ, the mind is the intangible essence that gives it direction, purpose, and meaning. Although the brain is a tangible organ with a complex network of neurons and synapses, in contrast, the mind is intangible which exists in the realms of thought, emotion and consciousness. Yet the mind directs the program or event of our lives, shapes our perceptions, influences our decisions, ultimately shaping who we are. The brain, with its billions of neurons and trillions of synapses, is a marvel of nature's design. It processes information, controls our movements and regulates bodily functions. But the mind gives the brain its power. The mind is never confined to the brain. It is a force that extends beyond the physical boundaries of our bodies and even beyond international boundaries, encompassing our thoughts, emotions, and consciousness. At the core of this relationship is the concept of neuroplasticity, the brain's extraordinary ability to reorganize itself by forming new neural connections. And this entire process is driven by our thoughts, emotions, feelings and experiences, which constantly reshape the brain's structure and function. In a sense the mind acts as a sculptor, moulding the brain over time to sculpt its neural pathways based on our habits, beliefs, and experiences.

Consider the example of Finius Gauge, a railroad worker who survived a severe brain injury in 1848, which dramatically changed his personality. Gauge was described as a responsible and reliable person before the accident. However, parts of his frontal lobe were damaged after a metal rod pierced his skull. At first he became impulsive and intemperate. Later, when he starts to believe that it was just an accident but he can start life anew by giving his future days a bigger purpose, his life starts to take a miraculous turn and he is subsequently appointed as a senior railway officer. His achievements continue to be smeared into people's mouths. Furthermore, studies have shown that our thoughts and emotions can directly affect the health and functioning of our brain. For example, chronic stress is associated with the shrinking of the hippocampus, which is directly involved in memory and learning. Conversely, mental development exercises increase gray matter density in brain areas associated with attention and emotional control, demonstrating the mind's power to shape brain structure and function. Mind enlightens the nature of consciousness, some theories suggest that consciousness arises from the interaction of neural networks, while others, in a holistic view, and see consciousness as a radical property of the universe. Above all, as we continue to unlock the power of our minds, we gain deeper insight into what it means to be human, providing new perspectives on the nature of consciousness and the essence of our existence.

Our mind is really mysterious, the more you know about it, the more interest and curiosity will increase, and writing about it may not be completed in two or three books. However, here I have written all the information you need to transform your adversities into massive success.

Now, I will come to the main topic where we shall know what actually happened, why do we feel helpless in front of several challenges! Why can't we use our mental power and resources at that time! The most important thing in this context is our 'mind-set'.

Unlocking Potential: Exploring The Power Of Mindset

'Your mind-set is the lens through which you view the world; adjust it to see endless possibilities and hidden opportunities.'

'Mind-set' is simply a set of beliefs, but it is much more than that. Apart from belief, it includes values, experience, Meta program, focus, decision, physiological state, mental state, etc. In very common language, it is also called point of view, and I call it 'colorful spectacles' on our eyes; the colors of the glasses are different for everyone. For example, you, I, Ritu, and Shulet wear glasses of red, blue, yellow and green respectively. Then if we are placed in front of a white object (which none of us have seen before) and asked what color the object is, then the color glasses we are wearing will see the object as that color accordingly. Is not it? Although the original color is white, you will see it as red, I will see blue, Ritu will see yellow and Shulet will see green. This may also cause disagreement and conflict between us. Again, if the glasses of the spectacles are rubbed or there is power in them, then no doubt one will see small, one will see big, one will see curved, one will see straight, some will see clearly, and some will see unclear.

Our mind-set is the glass that we are unconsciously familiar with, the glasses through which we see the world, see our situations, and see the events happening in front of us constantly. Now tell me, if the spectacle with which you are watching the events happening in front of you and happening to you are made of ground or rubbed glasses, different colors are applied, and abnormal power is given then how would the events look like? Just like that if your mind-set is passive i.e., you have shaky beliefs, your values and experiences are negative, if you mostly focus on negative things, if your mental and physical condition is not well, then won't fear arise in your mind? Can you be happy in life? Will your self-confidence not be shaken? Can you make the right decision? Can you see the possibilities? Will you get the mental strength you need to win? Will you have any inspiration to do something? No, never!

On the contrary, strong-minded personalities, i.e., those who have developed a strong and positive belief system, who always value their own success, their own growth, desire to learn, who know how to always stay positive, focus on positive aspects, who have been able to step out of their painful memories in life by taking the learning only, will they ever give up easily in the face of any problem? Such people can keep themselves in a resourceful state of mind in any situation in their lives even in adverse situations.

When the topic of 'state of mind' comes up, it is necessary to know that our mind-set directly affects our state of mind, that is, in which mental state you will be (unresourceful or resourceful) it completely depends on the mindset. If you believe that you can never get out of whatever problem you are going through, then automatically you will have fear in your mind, i.e., you will be in an unresourceful state of mind, and then your confidence will plummet, there will be no focus and attention to work, happiness will disappear from life. You will not be able to make good decisions, you will lose your creativity, you will lose motivation to work, above all you will lose your love for yourself, and your physiological condition will continue to deteriorate. On the contrary, a Strong Mind-set personality who knows how to put himself in a resourceful state of mind, is not afraid of anything easily, can naturally make good and powerful decisions, the power of creativity increased, can face any adversity with confidence. Go back to your own past and see the difference between the results of the things you did with confidence and the results of things you did out of fear! Check out how you behaved when you were happy! Think about how much better and faster you were able to complete a task when you were motivated in the past. And be sure, in the past, when you were confident in any work or when you were happy and joyful, got inspiration then these are your resources and still you have those in you, but maybe you are not able to realize it due to the pressure of the situation. If you find yourself in sadness and seek happiness, know that it resides within you. If loneliness weighs on your heart and you yearn for love, look within yourself, for love resides there too. In times of suffering, when peace eludes you, seek solace within yourself; it is where peace can be found. The courage and confidence needed to conquer fear are resources that lie within you. If illness, whether of the mind or body, afflicts you, remember that the power to heal resides within you as well. Your immune system, too, is a testament to your inherent strength. Despite these abundant inner resources provided by the Creator, we often fail to recognize and harness them, turning instead to external sources in our quest for relief from adversity.

The state of our mind plays a crucial role in managing physical discomforts such as pain, nausea, fatigue, depression, and irritability. When these symptoms manifest, our brain naturally releases endorphins, acting as a potent antidote. Furthermore, our mental state significantly influences vital bodily functions like digestion, blood circulation, respiration, and immune response through the autonomic nervous system—a natural, albeit complex, process devoid of magic or mystery.

For instance, sudden fear can spike blood circulation, yet the autonomic system maintains control. Similarly, irregular eating habits can disrupt digestion, but the mind holds the power to restore balance. In essence, our mind houses all the resources necessary to navigate and overcome life's challenges. Embracing this innate power requires cultivating a positive mind-set, enabling us to remain consistently resourceful.

'Resourceful state of mind turns obstacles into opportunities, challenges into stepping stones, and limitations into pathways to innovation.'

The Influence of Mind-set on Internal Representation and State of Mind

"Heaven is a state of mind, not a location." - Wayne Dyer

The state of one's mind holds significant importance. Sometimes it is said that, a state of mind is everything. The phrase "state of mind" encapsulates an individual's mental and emotional condition, influencing perceptions, decisions, and overall well-being. It reflects the harmony or turmoil within one's thoughts and feelings, shaping how they navigate life's challenges and opportunities. Therefore, cultivating a positive state of mind can greatly enhance one's quality of life and interactions with others.

Let's try to understand about state of mind in more detail. In fact, state of mind refers to a person's current state of mind or mood. State of mind is of two types: a resourceful state of mind and an unresourceful state of mind, resourceful state of mind ie love, joy, ecstasy, confidence, happiness etc. Conversely, unresourceful states of mind are fear, anger, sadness, loneliness, etc. It basically consists of two ingredients, the one is the personal internal representation and the other is the physiological state (of that particular moment). It will continue without discussing about Physiological state in detail, but personal internal representations should be understood. What we see, hear and feel is registered in our mind, that is, when an event from the external world is registered in our mind, then what we personally mean or give meaning to it in our mind is our personal internal representation. That is, it refers to a person's unique way of perceiving and interpreting the world around them. It involves an internal process through which people filter and organize external information to create their subjective reality. And this filter system on which the personal internal representation is formed directly influences by our mind set, because it directly influences the filter process.

Here's a little more about filters:

The filtration process refers to the way our mind processes and interprets events before storing them as memories or influencing our behavior. This process involves several steps, including deletion, distortion, and generalization, which shape our perception of reality. Here's a detailed explanation of this process with an example:

The Filtration Process

Sensory Input: Every event starts as sensory input—what we see, hear, feel, smell, or taste. This raw data is the initial information received by our senses.

1. **Deletion:** Our brain cannot process every piece of information we receive; it would be overwhelming. Deletion helps us focus by filtering out unnecessary details. For example, when you walk into a crowded room, you might only notice a friend's face among many others, ignoring the rest of the background noise and activity.
2. **Distortion:** This step involves altering the sensory input to fit our beliefs and experiences. Our minds might change or interpret the information differently to make it more understandable or meaningful. For instance, if someone waves at you from a distance and you can't see their face clearly, you might assume it's a friend based on their height and clothing, even if you're not entirely sure.
3. **Generalization:** Generalization simplifies our experiences by creating rules and patterns. This helps us navigate the world efficiently but can also lead to biases. For example, if

you've had several positive experiences with friendly dogs, you might generalize that all dogs are friendly and approachable.

Example of the Filtration Process

Imagine you're attending a party where you don't know many people. Here's how the filtration process might work:

Sensory Input:

As you walk into the party, you take in various sensory inputs: the sound of music, the sight of people mingling, the aroma of food, the feeling of the floor under your feet, and the taste of the drink in your hand.

Deletion:

Your mind can't process all these details simultaneously, so it deletes some of the less important (to you) information. You might focus on the faces of people around you, the conversation with the person next to you, and the layout of the room. You might not notice the color of the curtains, the specific background music playing, or the exact number of people in the room.

Distortion:

Your mind interprets the sensory input based on your past experiences and beliefs. For instance, if someone looks in your direction and then quickly turns away, you might distort this to mean they are avoiding you or are not interested in talking to you. This interpretation might be influenced by past experiences of feeling excluded.

Generalization:

You generalize based on patterns and rules created from previous experiences. If you've often felt uncomfortable in social settings, you might generalize that you don't do well at parties, leading you to feel anxious or shy. Conversely, if you've had positive social interactions, you might generalize that parties are enjoyable and people are generally friendly, making you feel more confident and open to meeting new people.

Conclusion

The filtration process in NLP shows how our mind selectively processes information, shaping our perception and reactions. When an event gets registered in our mind after filtration through all these process, it becomes our internal representation. And this internal representation varies from person to person, so it is called personal internal representation (PIR). Two people witnessing the same event can never interpret the same event equally because both people have different points of view, i.e., mind-set, and the internal representation that is formed in the mind is never the same. Whenever the meaning of the same event i.e., representation is different for different people, naturally the response to the same event can never be the same.

These personal internal representations combined with our emotions, thoughts and experiences directly affect our state of mind, i.e., our mood, and of course physiological state plays an important role in this. A person's state of mind or mood can fluctuate throughout the day depending on what they are thinking, feeling or experiencing at any given moment. And this state of mind produces our behavior, our behavior creates our actions, our actions determine our results.

I am trying to explain it to you with examples so you can understand logically. Suppose you are going to attend your dear friend's wedding and have been preparing for it for weeks. Very excitedly you are waiting for the day to come. You have completed your all sorts of preparations such as dress you will put on, which gift you will offer, how you will enjoy there etc... Finally the day you've been waiting for has arrived, but a few hours before the party started, you had a terrible headache. Now think about it and tell me in this situation, that is, with a severe headache, will that colorful party be same colorful for you? Even if the environment, people, food and drink, music, arrangement of the party are all the same, you cannot enjoy it well with such physiology; on the contrary, the music of the party may increase the discomfort for you. That is what! Here your physiological state directly controls your mental state, negative physiological state acts like a drop of kerosene on a pot full of cooked food.

On the contrary, you may have seen many times that you didn't feel well, you were sitting with down hearted all the day long, were sitting upset with your head bowed and hand on your cheek, you didn't even sense how long you have been sitting, suddenly you were startled by the voice of your dear friend. Even if you don't agree, he forcefully took you to a night party. Since you are upset, naturally you will not like the event going on there, but if you are forced to join the dance session with them, you will see that your mental state will start to change and you will regain a positive state of mind. That is what! When you were sitting at home thinking negative thoughts, you unconsciously acquired a physiological state to support negative thoughts, but whenever you joined a party, danced, your physiological state changed which made your mental state positive (At least temporarily).

When we are glad, happiness in our mind, automatically we smile, we don't have to smile thinking that 'I am happy, so now I have to smile!' Again, if we are sad, if we are in depression, if we suffer, then our eyes, face, and body are automatically affected, the body leans, and there is an impression of worry on the face and eyes. In fact, according to what is going on in our mind, unconsciously our physiology supports it, and that's why thought stayed in our mind, that is, if our physiological state does not support it, then the thought that is going on in our mind can never stay for long. Negative thoughts never come in positive physiological state.

We can learn how to easily shift ourselves from an unresourceful state of mind to a resourceful state of mind very quickly and can develop important unconscionable patterns to keep ourselves in a resourceful state most of the time. And only if we can achieve this important practice, we can change the outcome of our lives.

How to Shift Yourself from Unresourceful State Of Mind to Resourceful State Of Mind

Now let's see how we can change our unresourceful state of mind to a resourceful state of mind. Owing to this, I shall state the technique of rapid and the then solvation at first and then I shall share some tools and techniques for long term solutions with you.

QUICK FIX:

Our mind and body together form a system by which we are governed, so just as the mind affects the body directly, the physical state also can directly control the mental state. Although you cannot control the mind quickly consciously, you can take control of the physiological state consciously, which will change your mental state quickly. So whenever you feel that you are in an unresourceful state of mind, take direct control of your physical state.

The three to five minute technique you can do anytime especially when you feel the need. How to do it is explained step by step below-

1. Stand straight (if it is not possible to stand alone then sit straight), the spine, neck, head should be straight.
2. Widen the chest.
3. Take a long and deep breath and exhale, continue this process until the end.

4. Consciously bring a gentle smile to your face.
5. Hold yourself in this physiological state for three to five minutes without changing the gesture and posture.

Stop reading and apply it to yourself now to see how quickly your mood changes. However, it is never a long-term solution, for long-term solutions, that is, if you want to always keep yourself in a resourceful state of mind, then you must do exercises to make long-term changes in physical condition. All of the exercises I've mentioned here can increase blood flow, the release of endorphins and other mood-enhancing chemicals to the brain. Physiological changes can reduce stress, reduce symptoms of anxiety and depression, and improve overall mood or cognitive functioning.

Don't be alarmed by the name 'exercise' because I will suggest some very simple exercises that won't take much of your time, you just have to take the challenge of continuing it for at least 28 days without any breaks so that it automatically become your habitual pattern.

***The following technique must be done on an empty stomach;-

BOX BREATING:

One effective breathing exercise to maintain a resourceful state of mind is called "Box Breathing." Here's how you can do it:

- Find a quiet and comfortable place to sit or stand (The place outside the house, under the open sky or under the tree is better).
- Sit or stand with relaxed and take some slow deep breath and exhale.
- Now Close your eyes and take a deep breath in through your nose for a count of four. Feel your lungs fill with air.
- Hold your breath for a count of four.

- Slowly exhale through your mouth for a count of four, emptying your lungs completely.
- Hold your breath for another count of four before inhaling again.

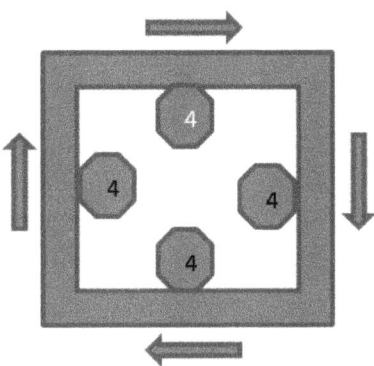

Repeat this cycle for several minutes, focusing on the rhythm of your breath and the sensations in your body.

Box breathing can help reduce stress and anxiety, increase your focus and concentration, and promote a calm and resourceful state of mind.

Box breathing, also known as square breathing, is a powerful technique that can help cultivate a strong mind-set by promoting relaxation, focus, and mental clarity. Here's how it can contribute to a strong mind-set:

- **Stress Reduction:** Box breathing activates the parasympathetic nervous system, which helps counteract the body's stress response. By focusing on your breath and slowing it down, you can reduce feelings of anxiety and stress, enabling you to approach challenges with a calmer mind-set.
- **Enhanced Focus:** The rhythmic nature of box breathing requires concentration, diverting your attention away from distracting thoughts. This practice can improve your ability to concentrate and stay focused on the task at hand,

essential for maintaining a strong mind-set in demanding situations.

- **<u>Improved Emotional Regulation:</u>** Regular practice of box breathing can help you become more aware of your emotions and better regulate them. This can prevent impulsive reactions and promote a more thoughtful and controlled response to difficult circumstances.
- **<u>Increased Resilience:</u>** By developing a consistent box breathing practice, you can enhance your resilience to stress and adversity. This technique teaches you to stay calm under pressure, bounce back from setbacks, and maintain a positive attitude, all of which are key components of a strong mind-set.
- **<u>Mind-Body Connection:</u>** Box breathing encourages mindfulness, which is the practice of being present in the moment. This heightened awareness of your body and breath can help you better understand your thoughts and emotions, leading to greater self-awareness and a stronger overall mind-set.

The rhythmic nature of box breathing requires concentration diverting your attention away from destructing thoughts. This practice can improve you your ability to cope with the challenges by developing your inner strength mostly this exercise will take 10 to 15 minutes. Incorporating box breathing into your daily routine can have profound effects on your mental and emotional well-being, ultimately helping you cultivate a strong and resilient mind-set that serves you well in all areas of life.

After completing this technique, shake the body lightly and warm-up and you can also drink a little water. Then you will go to the next exercise. This is also very simple. To do this exercise, you will need a skipping rope, which you must have with you from before. Choose a plane land and start skipping. If you are doing it for the first time then you should do it for at least twenty times, and take the target to increase the jump by five or ten more every day. If you're used to it, keep skipping until you're sweating and feel like you can't jump anymore, and commit to increasing the number of jumps gradually each day. If you feel uncomfortable with skipping rope for the first time, start with bare arms (without rope). Don't let excuses to come into your mind like 'I don't know how to skip or I don't have a skipping rope'. In the beginning, many obstacles may arise in the way, among them mental obstacles must have arisen because you are not familiar to do these. At first, you won't wake up, even if you do, you won't want to get out of bed. You may think that today is not a good day, so I will start tomorrow instead of today. Various excuses may arise in your mind like 'I didn't sleep well at night, my body is suffering today, etc.', because for your subconscious mind it is comfortable to sleep till late morning, not to exercise, no matter how bad it is for your future!

But in this case you have to take responsibility and consciously train your subconscious mind that sleeping late or not doing exercise is not comfortable for you at all, but doing exercise, waking up early in the morning -all this can give you a disease-free, stress-free, energetic and happy life! Be clear to yourself what are the disadvantages or the negative impact on life if you continue the way you are going and see what you will gain if you wake up early in the morning and make a habit of doing exercise. Think about its positive impacts in your life and the positive effects it has on your life, so that it is clear to your subconscious mind that sleeping for late morning and not doing exercises is never comfortable for you. And if not, like millions of other common people you'll set the alarm every morning, but when the alarm will ring you'll hit the snooze button and say to yourself, 'let me sleep for ten more minutes' or 'I'll start from tomorrow, not from today', those 10 minutes or tomorrow will never come!

Why Skipping or Jumping Is Most Important Exercise Basically When You Are In Adversities

Skipping, or jump, offers numerous benefits for both the mind and body. Here are some reasons why it is important:

Physical Health Benefits

1. Cardiovascular Fitness: Skipping is an excellent cardio workout that strengthens the heart, improving cardiovascular health and endurance.
2. Weight Loss: It burns a significant number of calories, aiding in weight loss and fat reduction.
3. Muscle Toning: Regular skipping tones muscles in the legs, core, and arms, enhancing overall muscle strength and definition.
4. Coordination and Balance: The rhythm and timing required in skipping improve coordination, balance, and agility.
5. Bone Health: The impact of skipping helps improve bone density, reducing the risk of osteoporosis.

Skipping is a highly effective exercise for jolting the entire body, promoting overall physical activity that can aid in digestive health. The rhythmic movement involved in skipping stimulates the muscles in the abdomen, which can help to relieve trapped gas and reduce symptoms of acidity. By encouraging better blood circulation and increasing the body's metabolism, skipping supports efficient digestion and helps to alleviate discomfort associated with gas and acidity. Regular skipping can thus contribute to a healthier digestive system and improved overall well-being.

Mental Health Benefits

1. Stress Reduction: Physical exercise like skipping releases endorphins, which are natural mood lifters, helping to reduce stress and anxiety.

2. Cognitive Function: The coordination required in skipping engages the brain, enhancing cognitive function and mental sharpness.
3. Boosts Confidence: Achieving goals in skipping, such as a higher number of jumps, can boost self-esteem and confidence.
4. Mindfulness and Focus: Skipping requires concentration on timing and rhythm, promoting mindfulness and helping to clear the mind.
5. Energy and Mood: Regular exercise increases overall energy levels and improves mood, contributing to a positive state of mind.

Incorporating daily exercise into the routine offers many mental and emotional benefits that contribute to a more resourceful state of mind and increase productivity, increase mental clarity, reduce stress, improve mood and increase energy levels and an overall better quality of life. Regular physical activity leads to more focused, creative and productive days. Almost everyone knows these things consciously but despite that there is a huge deficiency in applying them in their own life. People think that once the situation turns in their favor, if they can get rid of the obstacles, then they will start to do these things, and wait for the time to change. So whether I'm in my counselling sessions or in my mental wellness mastery program, I ask all participants that what I am teaching and sharing are not to follow after changing the situation rather to transform the situation in favour of you. You will have to do to bring the situation in your favor of you without delay, start applying it from the moment you learned it.

'Today' is the golden moment where every good deed finds its perfect beginning, turning ordinary days into auspicious days. Start today...'

The Blueprint for a Growth Mindset

We have already learned that the state of mind at a particular moment and our physiological state at that particular moment are directly controlled or produced by our thought process or perception (i.e., PIR). Therefore, by simply changing the physiological state, it may not be possible to always have a resourceful state, because whenever a negative thought comes to mind or we face a negative situation, we move into an unresourceful state because of our negative PIR. Since personal internal representation is formed based on your mindset then you must work on your mindset along with physiology, because your thought process, perception, feelings, emotions are influenced by your mind-set (i.e., your beliefs, values, experiences, focus, meta program, decision etc.). Here I will discuss in detail how to develop a strong and growth mind-set and share some important techniques that are very powerful yet simple. Before that you must know how this mind-set is developed, why I compared it to the 'artificial glasses' we wear!

When we are born in this world, our memory files are almost empty, that is, like the RAM, ROM or hard disks of an unused new computer, there is nothing in it except some inbuilt system.

So a child does not understand about religion, about failure-success, they do not have any negative thoughts, any doubt, and any ego. Even a child knows nothing about himself, who he is, where he comes from, whether he is good or bad! They never suffer from insecurity or inferiority. In fact, because their rational mind is not formed in childhood, they never think in complex ways like adults. And because of all these reasons, a child never suppresses or can keep hide his natural emotions inside him; the reactions of his inner world burst out then and there. A child's mind-set is usually one of curiosity, innocence and openness to the world around them, so they are almost always (unless normal processes are disrupted) in a resourceful state of mind. That is, there is no artificiality in the child's mentality, so he is much braver. Here I am definitely talking about children less than 3 years, children of this age usually get love, care, laughter, importance from their parents and relatives.

Then when a child gradually grows up, parents, relatives start to scare, compare with other children, scold, and in most cases the child does not understand why he is being bullied. Apart from parents and relatives they also get such input from teachers and elders. "You are not perfect, you are not worthy enough, you are lazy, you cannot do anything, my son is naughty, fickle, only one can be first in school, you are less intelligent, 'X' is much better at studies than you, you are stupid, you are ass, you are crazy," all these are tagged with the child's identity. When they gradually grown up these types of comments are also increasing, and with these insultation, negligence, rejection, negative talk such as "life is very hard and complex, it is not easy to earn money, money is the root of evil, our society is not good etc." are also added. Naturally, the mind-set changes, the self-identity is lost and the 'projected self' is formed, where the ego, fear of failure, anger, sadness, suffering, lack of confidence, negative thoughts, hatred, low self-image, co-dependency, and blaming all are nourished unknowingly in his mind.

Naturally, when a child becomes an adult, his mentality changes almost completely, he can no longer believe how valuable he really is in this world, what infinite power is hidden in himself, he loses his importance to himself, begins to doubt him. Lose focus on solutions and learn to focus more on problems. Rather than winning, the mentality of accepting defeat, giving up or not participating is created. Focusing on failure leads to feelings of frustration and loss of motivation, make mistakes or refrains from taking decisions due to excessive caution and fear, all of these increases obstacles by limiting his willpower and mentality.

In the journey of life, many of us find ourselves trapped in roles and identities shaped by societal expectations, family influences, and environmental factors. These projected self often create a facade that disconnects us from our true essence. Only by breaking free from these artificial identities can we realize and enjoy our real resources and power. This journey towards self-realization requires knowing and understanding the real self. Here, we will explore several important and powerful tools and techniques that can help you discover your true self.

The Importance of Knowing the Real Self

Understanding your real self is crucial for several reasons:

1. **Authenticity:** When you know your true self, you can live authentically, making choices that align with your core values and desires.
2. **Fulfilment:** Living in alignment with your true self leads to a deeper sense of satisfaction and fulfilment.
3. **Empowerment:** Understanding your strengths, weaknesses, and unique qualities empowers you to harness your true potential.

The Journey Within: Exploring Self-Love as a Pathway to Discover Your True Self

Self-Love Technique is the magic mantra to find your own self. Look, to survive in life, you will have to do many things, have to engage in relationships, have to maintain sociology, have to be busy for earnings, to plan for the future, but in the midst of everything, people forget one thing, that is to love and take care of themselves. What is the value or fulfilment of what you are doing and what for you are doing if you are not well or healthy! You have to think and understand that there is only one person in your life who will accompany you from your birth to your last breath, that person is none other than you; no other person in this world can accompany you throughout your life, even if they want to. If you failed to pay attention to you or to love yourself due to the pressure of work, activities or taking care of others, your real-self will naturally be destroyed. What you love or whom you love will gradually disappear one by one from your life, or you will not feel fulfilled in life despite of all this.

Many scholars misrepresent self-love as it is selfishness! Tell me one thing, if you don't take steps to keep you well, to keep you healthy, how will you take responsibility to take care of others or love others?

Let's listen to a beautiful story to understand how important self-love is, especially in finding your real-self:

Once upon a time in a quaint village there lived a young lady named Niva. Niva was known for her kindness and willingness to help others, but she always neglected herself. She used to spend her days by taking care of her family, friends and neighbours, she never spare even a moment to meet her own need. Niva's life continued like this, she was very happy by taking care of others, loving everyone and doing benefit to others. She enjoyed the times during the day as long as she could engage with all of these. She always put others before herself and gave importance more than herself. Despite her warm heart she often felt lonely and unsatisfied. She constantly sought validation from the people around her, believing that their approval would fill her inner emptiness, but it never did. At the end of the day, when everyone was at home, Niva felt lonely and unsatisfied even among with her family members.

One day while walking through the forest, Niva stumbled upon an ancient mirror hidden among the roots of a tree. Intrigued by its ornate frame and the soft glow emanating from it, she decided to take it home. She didn't even know that it was enchanted and held the wisdom of ancient times.

That night when Niva felt lonely and unsatisfied, she looked into the mirror hoping to find solace, the mirror astonished her and said, "Niva" - it said in a soft voice, "The answers you seek, the emptiness you seek to escape from, are not in the approval of others but within yourself, to discover your real-self you must learn to love yourself."

A confused but curious Niva seemed to ask herself, "How can I love myself when I feel so imperfect?"

The mirror replied, "Self-love is like nurturing a seed of full potential within you. It requires self-care, giving values to yourself, and belief in your worth, rediscovering your own strength, and forgiving yourself for mistakes."

Niva was shocked and thought that she had never really focused on self-discovery, she had Seek the company of others in loneliness, but never accompanied herself! That's why she feels lonely even in the crowd; her heart seems always to be empty.

Gradually Niva started to experience profound changes in her since she started practicing self-love. She was succeeded to discover her hidden talents and passions that she never focused before and through this process she realized the power of her authentic self-creation and a person full of limitless potential.

Niva's new self-love, self-discovery has not only changed her life but also inspired many people around her.

The moral of the story is that self-love is never selfishness; it is essential. By nurturing and loving ourselves we unlock our true potential and inspire others to do the same leading to more fulfilling and authentic lives.

Because people don't love themselves, even in today's modern era many signboards are hanging on roadsides, railway platforms or various public places with cautionary words, "Watch and cross the road", "Smoking kills you", "Don't drive while drunk", -etc. Self-love is actually developing a deep relationship with one's soul, understanding one's emotions and feelings correctly. Self-love is never selfishness and egoism is never self-love. From an early age a child is taught at home or at school to love others and be philanthropic. But 'love yourself' is rarely used or taught. So it is not possible for common people to understand the importance of self-love. From the moment you start loving yourself, your life will take on a different dimension, momentum will return to life, positive changes will come in life. Surprisingly, you will notice that all the things that seemed very complicated are becoming easy and simple, how sweet the relationships are becoming. You can always feel happy, calm and energetic in yourself.

Additional Importance of Self-Love:-

1. Self-love helps you to live a happy life.
2. Self-love can help you to get rid of mental and physical ailments and keeps away from these.
3. Self-love helps to keep away from any bad habits, eating unhealthy food and addiction.
4. It increases self-awareness and helps to take correct and effective decisions.
5. It gives inner peace.

6. Self-love leads to tremendous improvement in interpersonal and personal relationships.
7. It helps to a great extent to overcome mental obstacles such as anxiety, unnecessary fear, depression, sadness, loneliness.
8. It acts as a sleep inducer.

How to Build Self-Love:-

(A) Mirror Exercise; The Five Minute Rule to Reflect Your True Self:

This technique is one of my favorites which have brought about the most significant changes in my life during difficult times. You will never realize the miracles this small, simple yet powerful technique can do in your life if you don't practice it. I stated step by step process here, definitely feel free to practice it, you will get the results very soon. Do it before going to bed at night.

Steps:

1. Wash your face, hands and feet well with normal cold water and get fresh.

2. Stand straight in front of a clean mirror keeping your backbone and neck straight and widen your chest.
3. Look at yourself directly from top to bottom in the mirror.
4. Take slow and deep breaths through your nose, and slowly exhale through your mouth (Do it for 5 times).
5. Keep your eyes straight towards the eyes in the front mirror.
6. Say the following sentences with sincere feelings; never take it lightly, or merely 'words for words' sake. Because remember that feelings are very important to your subconscious mind, it always tries to manifest whatever says and does with great feelings. So recite with feelings; - 'I love my self', 'I thank myself' and 'I bless myself'.

Repeat the sentences 7 to 10 times, the more you recite the more the feeling will generate.

(B) Inner Radiance Discovery: Unveiling Your Unique Qualities

In the journey of life, we often seek external validation and recognition, hoping to find happiness and fulfilment through the approval of others. Yet, true contentment and profound satisfaction lie not in the outer world but within us. The concept of 'Inner Radiance Discovery' invites us to embark on an introspective exploration, guiding us to uncover and embrace our unique qualities—the very essence of who we are.

Inner radiance is the light that shines from within, illuminating our path and influencing those around us. It is the manifestation of our true self, unhindered by societal expectations or external pressures. When we discover and nurture our inner radiance, we unlock a wellspring of potential, creativity, and resilience. This journey is about recognizing and celebrating the distinct traits that make us who we are, understanding that each individual possesses a unique combination of strengths, talents, and passions.

Finding our own qualities requires us to look inward with honesty and compassion. It involves acknowledging our strengths and weaknesses, understanding our values and beliefs, and embracing our experiences and aspirations. This self-discovery process is not about perfection but about authenticity—embracing ourselves as we are and recognizing the beauty in our individuality.

The path to inner radiance discovery is transformative. As we delve deeper into understanding ourselves, we cultivate self-awareness and self-acceptance. We begin to see how our unique qualities contribute to our overall well-being and how they can positively impact our relationships, careers, and communities. This inner work fosters a sense of purpose and direction, empowering us to live authentically and align our actions with our true selves.

In this exploration of inner radiance, I will delve into various practices and techniques to help you uncover and nurture your unique qualities. Each step will bring you closer to understanding and embracing your inner light.

As we embark on this journey together, remember that the discovery of your inner radiance is a lifelong process. It is a continual unfolding of your true self, a journey of growth and transformation. Embrace the process with an open heart and mind, knowing that each step brings you closer to a deeper understanding of who you are and the unique qualities that make you shine.

Welcome to the path of Inner Radiance Discovery. May this journey illuminate your true self and inspire you to live a life of authenticity, purpose, and fulfilment.

One effective technique for discovering and nurturing your inner radiance is maintaining a Daily Qualities Journal. This practice involves writing down three unique qualities you recognize in yourself each day for 28 days. By consistently focusing on your strengths, talents, and positive attributes, you will cultivate a deeper understanding and appreciation of your unique qualities.

How to Practice the Daily Qualities Journal

1. **Prepare Your Journal**: Choose a dedicated notebook or digital journal for this practice. Having a specific place to record your thoughts will help you stay organized and committed.
2. **Set a Daily Time**: Find a time each day that works best for you to reflect and write. This could be in the morning to start your day with positivity or in the evening as a way to wind down and reflect on your day.
3. **Write Three Qualities**: Each day, take a few moments to write down three qualities you appreciate about yourself. These can be anything from personal traits, skills, achievements, or actions you've taken. For example:
   - "I am compassionate and always willing to help others."
   - "I have a strong work ethic and am dedicated to my projects."
   - "I am creative and come up with innovative solutions."
4. **Be specific and Reflective**: Try to be specific about each quality. Reflect on recent experiences or actions that demonstrate these qualities. This reflection helps reinforce the positive aspects of yourself and provides concrete examples of your strengths.
5. **Avoid Repetition**: Challenge yourself to come up with new qualities each day. This encourages you to dig deeper and recognize a broader range of attributes, preventing you from relying on the same few qualities repeatedly.

6. **Review Your Entries**: At the end of each week, review your entries. Notice any patterns or recurring themes. Reflect on how these qualities have impacted your life and interactions with others.

7. **Celebrate Your Progress**: After completing the 28 days, take some time to celebrate your progress. Acknowledge the growth in your self-awareness and the positive impact this practice has had on your self-esteem and inner radiance.

Now you might be wondering what good qualities you have that are worth writing down! Actually, we all have many good qualities and you have many too, but instead of focusing on them, we usually focus more on our imperfections and weaknesses and when we think about them again and again, our self-image decreases and then we afraid to face any obstacles or problems. If you don't face obstacles or problems directly because of fear, you will never win; you will never succeed in life.

If you write down your good qualities on a daily basis, your self-confidence will automatically increase; you will never feel down in front of anyone or in front of any problem. Not only that, many new paths will open before your eyes, many opportunities will be opened which can take your life to a higher level. You may also discover some qualities that make you one of the best!

I am trying to make you understand through a small story about how the power of good qualities of a person can bring his success too high by overcoming prohibition and opposition.

The Successful Journey of Bishwa:

A young man named Bishwa lived in a small town located at the foot of the hill. He was an average student, not good at athletics or sports at all. It is to say the least he was shadowed by the skills of his more accomplished peers. Bishwa harboured dreams of success but his confidence was constantly eroded by self-doubt and comparison.

While browsing the local library one day, Bishwa's eyes were caught by an old dusty book called "The Hidden Power Within". Intrigued, he opened it and read a passage that would change his life forever. "Write down the good qualities you see in yourself, for in these words lie the seeds of your strength and success."

Inspired, Bishwa decided to start a unique experiment. Every day he carried a small notebook and diligently recorded the positive qualities he saw in himself. At first it was difficult though - he struggled to find more than a few kind words for himself, but as the days turned into weeks, miracles began to happen.

Bishwa began to notice moments of kindness, inspiration and sparks of creativity in his daily life. He wrote about his own boundless patience, unwavering loyalty and growing determination. With each entry Bishwa felt a subtle yet profound change within him. As the inferiority complex is removed, Bishwa learns to see and appreciate his own strengths, his confidence grows and he begins to believe in his potential. The practice of writing down these qualities actually acts like a mirror for Bishwa, reflecting the best parts of himself and helping him develop a resilient and positive mind-set.

One evening when he was reviewing his notebooks he wondered to himself, 'despite of having so many qualities in him he has been suffering from self-doubt! Bishwa realized that he had filled the pages with his various talents and qualities - which he now recognized in himself, and then he took bold decisions. Bishwa, with new inner strength, decided to pursue his long-held dream of starting his own business.

Bishwa started a small but innovative technology start-up by taking from the qualities he had carefully documented. He instilled in his company the values of integrity, dedication and creativity, by which he was admired and written about.

Years have passed and the start-up has grown into a thriving enterprise. He is now an example to the people. People are amazed to see how an ordinary young man turned his life around and achieved extraordinary success! Now in his interviews and speeches Bishwa often shares the secret of his success. He credits his success to the simple yet profound practice of writing good qualities. He explained how this practice not only helped him find his inner strength but also developed a mind-set that attracts success and positivity.

Bishwa's own journey of self-discovery proves that by knowing and understanding ourselves we can discover a powerful inner strength. This power instills our confidence, guides our actions and ultimately leads us to extraordinary success.

So why are you delaying? From today, from this moment pick up a pen and a notebook and start the journey of your self-discovery and prove that you are one of the best!

Believe is Power

Belief is the most important ingredient of mind-set and it is said that "If you have nothing but believe you can achieve". Beliefs are considered a key component of our internal map of reality. It represents a person's personal perception of truth or falsity and influences thoughts, emotions and behavior. Beliefs are formed through past experiences, cultural influences and personal interpretations.

Beliefs can be empowering or limiting, empowering believes support personal growth, motivation and positive outcomes. When beliefs are limiting it hinders progress and can create barriers to success. Our goal is to identify limiting beliefs and transform them into empowering ones by breaking them down. Beliefs are deeply rooted in the subconscious mind which directly affects our mind set as well as our state of mind in various ways.

Perception of Reality: - Beliefs shape how we interpret events and situations. If we believe that challenges are opportunities for growth, we can often face them with an open and proactive mind-set. Conversely if we believe that challenges are our insurmountable obstacles we can feel defeated and anxious.

Emotional Response: - Our beliefs directly affect our emotions. Positive beliefs can lead to confidence, optimism and motivation, whereas negative beliefs can lead to fear, anxiety and depression. For example, believing in the ability to succeed increases inner strength and enthusiasm.

Behavior and Action (Depends on state of Mind):- Beliefs drive our behavior and decisions. Empowering beliefs encourage us to take action, persevere, and embrace new opportunities. On the other hand limiting beliefs can lead to procrastination, avoidance and self-sabotage.

Self-Identity:- Beliefs play an important role in our self-concept and identity. If we believe that we are capable and worthy, we develop a lasting sense of self-esteem and self-worth. Negative beliefs can result in a lack of self-esteem and confidence.

Interpersonal relationship: - Beliefs affect how we interact with others and how quickly we can build rapport. Positive beliefs about people and relationships can lead to trust, cooperation and healthy communication. Negative beliefs can result in mistrust, conflict and bad relationships.

Problem solving and creativity: - An open and positive belief system enhances our ability to think creatively and solve problems effectively. Believing in the potential of solutions and new ideas encourages innovative thinking and adaptability.

Here is a beautiful example of The Power of Believing.

The Power of Beliefs; A Transformative Journey:-

Once upon a time there lived a man named Samuel in the bustling city of Metropolis. Samuel always considered himself to be an average person, because the middle-class family he grew up in, the environment, the people, even his parents —whatever he experienced, whatever he learned from everyone never made him a confident person, he never believed that he is unique and has infinite power hidden within him.

He worked a mundane job in a local factory. His days were filled with repetitive work and his evenings numbed by the fatigue of the day were spent in front of the television. He believed in his heart that he had little to gain from life and was destined for a middle-class life.

One day when Samuel was coming home from work, he passed by a new bookstore that had just opened. Intrigued, he wandered inside and looked at the shelves and suddenly his eyes caught on a brightly colored book. Curious Samuel immediately decided to buy the book and started reading that night.

The book talks about the incredible power of beliefs and how they shape our reality. It explains that "empowering beliefs can change one's mind-set and ultimately change one's life". Samuel was skeptical but decided to apply this reading to his own life. He understood that he has nothing to lose but if he gets something!

The first chapter was about identifying limiting beliefs; What Samuel learned was that he had many limiting beliefs: "I'm not smart enough", "I'm too old to change", and "Success is for others, not for me". The book guided him to challenge these beliefs and replace them with empowering ones: "I am capable of learning and growing", "It's never too late to start over", and "I deserve success just like anyone else".

As he began to accept the beliefs, he noticed subtle changes in his attitude and behavior. He started taking night classes to improve his skills, forgetting the tiredness of returning from work, which he had never considered before. His newfound belief in his own potential boosted his motivation. Slowly but surely he began to excel in his studies and even discovered a passion for engineering.

His new skills and confidence became the stepping stone to his workplace promotion. He keeps challenging himself, setting higher goals and pursuing them with long-term determination. His empowering beliefs transformed his mind-set from scarcity and limitation to abundance and possibility.

Years passed and Samuel's life changed dramatically. He rose to a leadership role in the company earning respect and admiration from his colleagues. He also became a role model mentor, encouraging others to believe in themselves and follow their dreams.

One bright evening Samuel was invited to give a talk about his journey at a local community event. As he stood on stage he looked into the faces of the audience and saw images of his former self trapped by their circumstances, completely unaware of the true power within them. "Beliefs," Samuel began, "are the foundations of our lives. They shape our thoughts, our actions, and ultimately our reality. When we choose to believe in our potential, we unlock a world of possibilities. Empowering beliefs have the power to change our mind-set, our state of mind, and our lives in ways we never imagined."

Samuel's story spread throughout Metropolis, inspiring countless individuals to challenge their limiting beliefs and embrace the power within. The city flourished with newfound creativity, innovation, and success, all sparked by the simple yet profound act of changing one's beliefs.

And so, Samuel's life became a testament to the transformative power of empowering beliefs, proving that with the right mind-set, anyone can achieve greatness and create a life filled with purpose and fulfilment.

Transform Your Life: A Comprehensive Guide to Change Beliefs

Belief generally refers to a state of accepting something as true or real, often without absolute proof. It involves confidence in the truth, existence, or reliability of something, whether it's a concept, idea, person, or phenomenon. Beliefs can be based on personal experiences, cultural upbringing, teachings, evidence, or a combination of these factors.

Beliefs play a fundamental role in shaping individual perspectives, behaviors, and decisions. They can range from religious or spiritual convictions to scientific theories, political ideologies, or personal convictions about morality and ethics.

It's important to note that beliefs can vary greatly among individuals and societies, and they are subject to change over time with new experiences, knowledge, or evidence that challenges or reinforces them. Thus, beliefs are not necessarily fixed or universal but are integral to how individuals make sense of the world around them. Most of the time, we accept certain beliefs (limiting beliefs) that harm us are based on misconceptions and we accept those beliefs without asking ourselves, 'What is the basis of what I accept or believe? Are these universal truths?' For example, you believe that your problems will never end in your life and this belief has developed because whenever you set out to do something, you face or have faced some obstacle. Various past experiences of yours have strengthened this belief. But if I ask, is it a universal truth like "the sun rises in the east"? Of course not! That means your answer will be "no"! If I ask you more questions, 'Have you had problems in all areas of life, especially when you went to do something?' - Check inside your mind and the answer will be "No"! Right? So see, what you started to believe to be the eternal truth and had a profound negative impact on your life is nothing more than your misconception or superstition. Yes or no? Here's how I broke your misconceptions or limiting beliefs? By asking questions! If you question your beliefs correctly, the negative beliefs will break down. If you can't break your negative or limiting beliefs, you'll never be able to adopt positive and empowering beliefs. I will first explain step by step how to break negative or limiting beliefs and then explain how to adopt positive and empowering beliefs that will help you see a world of possibilities.

With a cool head, first take a pen and paper and write down what negative beliefs you have that are actually limiting you, blocking your path to success.

1. While writing, the list can become long, but write everything carefully.
2. Once you've written them all down, pick one of them, let's say the first belief you want to break is "I can never achieve great success!"
3. Then ask yourself the following questions;-

    (A) Is this universal truth?

    (A) What logic do I have in its support?

    (B) What is the evidence for and against this belief?

        i. What proof do I have that supports this belief?

        ii. What proof do I have that contradicts this belief?

    (C) How did I come to hold this belief?

        i. When did I first start believing this?

        ii. Who or what influenced me to adopt this belief?

    (D) What are the consequences of holding these beliefs?

        i. How does this belief impact my life (both positive and negative)?

        ii. What opportunities have I missed because of this belief?

    (E) How would my life be different if I did not hold this belief?

        i. What action would I take if I no longer believed this?

    ii. How my feelings and behaviour change?

(F) What past experiences have reinforced this belief? Are there specific events that have made this belief strong?

(G) What behaviours or habit do I have the keep this believe alive?

(H) What fears are associated with letting go of this belief?
    i. What am I afraid might happen if I stop believing this?
    ii. How realistic are these fears?

Take time to answer each question thoughtfully; Write your response to clarify your thoughts.

Beliefs (whether negative or limiting) every belief is like a moat, a giant wall standing on a strong foundation surrounding us. We think that walled moat protects us, but it doesn't, in fact, they keep us trapped in a blind well, from which we cannot get out and experience the world of possibilities and we limit ourselves. So to break all those beliefs and enter the world of possibilities, its foundations must be shaken first and this is possible only through the right questions. By systematically questioning and analyzing your limiting beliefs, you can weaken their hold on your psyche and make room for more empowering beliefs that support growth and success.

Let's now look at how to develop empowering beliefs while breaking down limiting beliefs, which will help you break out of the limiting trenches of your life and unleash the world's vast possibilities.

To develop imperialist beliefs you need to ask yourself the following questions;

a. What else can I believe instead (the old limiting believe) that can help me?

b. What new belief would better serve my goals and well-being?

c. What belief aligns with the person I want to become?
d. How would adopting the new belief positively impact my life?
e. What evidence supports this new belief?
f. Can I find example in my own life or others' lives where this belief is true?
g. What achievements or success can I attribute to adopting this belief?
h. What values and strings support this new belief?
i. How does this new belief align with my core values how will this new believe change my self-identity?
j. What obstacle might I face in adopting this belief, and how can I overcome them?
k. How will this new belief influence my relationships and all areas of my life?

You may think that why it is necessary to ask so many questions in the game of breaking and building beliefs! Actually questioning is necessary so that you can satisfy your logical mind and only then that belief can be implanted in your subconscious mind, otherwise you have to move with shaky beliefs that can crumble to dust for any small reason. You can never rise to the top of success with a stair of shaky belief. Now think about how you can strengthen the ladder of Empowering Beliefs that you need to build to ensure your success, how you can practice them so that they become ingrained in your heart, what steps you can take to embody the new beliefs! Maybe you can do affirmations or write them down every day or find strong evidence to support them, the choice is yours. But if you really want an unprecedented transformation in life, then there is no other way but to do these. You have to decide whether you will start five to ten years from now, or start applying today!

CHAPTER-4

PART-2 Unshackling Consciousness: Liberating the Mind's Virus

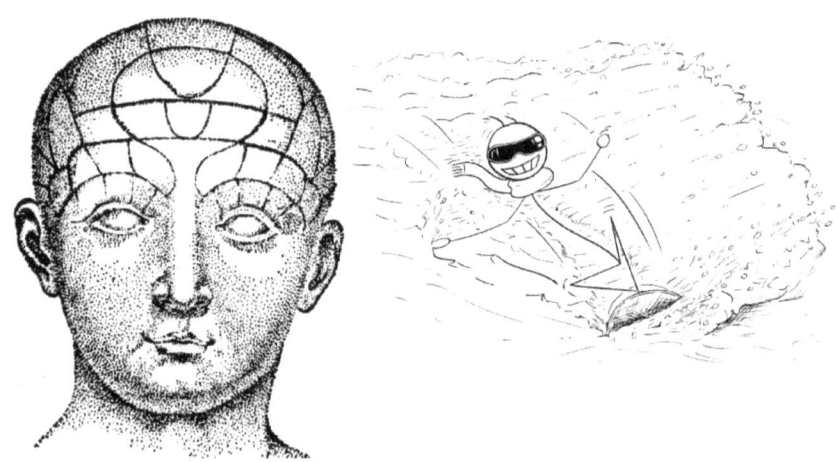

In this digital age our minds are bombarded with an overwhelming flow of information, much of which is negative, confusing or simply irrelevant. Just as a computer can be infected with a virus that corrupts its functionality, our mind can be infected with harmful thoughts, beliefs and attitudes that not only hinder our growth and our success but also negatively affect our basic lifestyle. These mental intrusions, which we may call 'mind viruses', enter our subconscious mind, shaping our perceptions and directing our actions, often without our conscious awareness.

Mind viruses are insidious, if left unchecked they can manifest as self-doubt, fear, procrastination, negative thinking, and negative self-talk among other forms. These psychological aggressors can destroy our confidence, stifle our creativity and destroy our ambitions. The good news is that much like computer virus, 'mind viruses' can be identified, quarantined and eradicated.

In this phase we will explore the nature of viruses of the mind, how they take deeply rooted and spread in the soil of our minds. We will uncover the subtle ways in which they influence our thoughts and behaviors, even though they may be disguised as seemingly harmful or familiar patterns. Most importantly I will equip you with practical strategies and techniques to clear your mind of these harmful influences and help you develop a mind-set that is extremely strong, positive and primed for success.

I try to listen and understand the problems of my participants especially those who are suffering from anxiety, depression, phobia, fear, over thinking, stress, etc. and I advise them not to consume any negative, unnecessary distracting and irrelevant content at all. In that case, almost everyone's opinion is "I know they're very harmful for me, I really want to get rid of them, I've tried so hard but I can't get rid of them, it's like a habit without doing I feel something is missing, I feel like I'm addicted, I feel bored all day." - It's true, if you get addicted to something and you don't do it, you won't spend time, you'll get bored, you'll get depressed, you might feel lonely. And that is why understanding our transcendental mind is so important.

If I explain through a moral story, you will understand very easily;

In the bustling town of Thoughts Villa, there lived a young man named Leo. Leo was known far and wide for his intelligence and creativity, but he had a tendency to get distracted easily. His mind was always racing with ideas, but if he didn't keep it busy with meaningful work, it would often lead him into doing irrelevant things.

One day, as Leo was walking through the town square, he noticed a strange creature causing a commotion. It was a peculiar monster with bright, colorful fur and a mischievous glint in its eyes. The monster seemed to be busy straightening the tails of dogs passing by, much to the confusion of the animals.

Intrigued, Leo approached the monster and asked why it was doing such a strange thing. The monster replied, "My dear boy, my mind is one of the busiest thing in this universe. If I don't keep it busy in relevant work, it will keep me busy in irrelevant work, like straightening a dog's tail."

Leo was struck by the monster's words. He realized that he, too, was often at the mercy of his own busy mind. He would start projects with great enthusiasm, only to abandon them halfway through for the next shiny idea that crossed his mind.

Determined to change his ways, Leo decided to focus on one project at a time, giving it his full attention and dedication. As he did so, he found that his mind became more disciplined and focused. He no longer wasted time on irrelevant tasks but instead channelled his energy into work that was meaningful and fulfilling.

In the end, Leo learned that the mind is indeed one of the busiest thing in the universe, but by keeping it engaged in relevant work, one can harness its power for greatness. And so, he became a shining example in Thoughts Ville, inspiring others to do the same.

Now say, you have a powerful genie that is always ready to do anything for your good and waiting to act on your command, can you give that powerful genie the right task, the task that makes your life beautiful? Whenever you can't or don't do that, naturally, in its usual way, it keeps you busy in addictive activities to make you feel comfortable, to get temporary pleasure. I have also found participants who, after working all the day, are so engrossed in watching that negative content till two or three in the morning that they don't even notice the time. Try to understand very well, every person in this world is allotted 24 hours of time in a day, no one gets a second more and no one gets less. 24 hours allotted to every human being from child to old, rich to poor, successful to unsuccessful, very ordinary to highly successful. But - but do you know what really makes the difference between ordinary and extraordinary? - Based on how long and how you are using the infinitely powerful 'genie' located in your brain during this twenty-four hour period. Extraordinary personalities are not born extraordinary, their thoughts, their actions, their every step makes them extraordinary. You may be familiar with the name Clonal Sanders, founder of Kentucky Fried Chicken (KFC)! Did his father know Colonel Sanders was extraordinary when his father died at the age of six, leaving him to cook and take care of his younger siblings? - 'No' never! But Colonel Sanders fought with various complex situations of life and managed to register himself as one of the most successful personalities of the world at an almost old age only by channelling his precious time into constructive thinking. Despite facing numerous rejections he remained steadfast in his belief in his recipe and vision. He has spent years refining his cooking techniques and recipes, focusing his thoughts on creating a delicious and unique dish.

So I say have faith that you too can become one of the best in the world no matter what your situation is, what your age is or whatever problem you are in. But you have to learn to use your powerful 'Genie' i.e., your mind properly during most of the 24 hours allotted to you each day.

So let's see now how you can use the 24 hours allotted to you daily for constructive work in a highly structured way so that various negative viruses do not get a chance to enter inside your mind and for these the most important thing is making daily schedule. Remember if you don't know what you will do in the next 1 hour then that one hour will be wasted from your precious time of your life, if you don't know what you will do in the next 24 hours then you won't even understand when that precious day will be gone from your life. So to give proper value to the most precious time of life, there must be day schedule. You might say that "I have a fixed schedule of daily activities, I have to stick to that routine and I stick to it," then the following lines are definitely for you.

First: The schedule currently you are maintaining will give you the same results you are currently getting.

Second: Ask yourself, if someone else is forcing you to maintain this daily schedule, or are you forcing yourself to maintain it yourself?

Third: Be sure that if you find time in your daily schedule to consume negative content, then it's time to change that day schedule right now.

Fourth: My question is how many times have you had daily routine, monthly routine or such routine but failed to follow that routine regularly?

Let me now discuss how to make day schedule in a structured way so that you can enjoy every day, every moment and use your precious time properly to destroy problems and reveal the path to success. Make your day schedule in a step by step process as I have explained here, I promise you will not find it difficult to follow the schedule, nor you will fail to follow it, and you will definitely reap the benefits in the near future.

STEPS:-

(A) Make a day schedule in the evening or shortly before going to sleep.

(B) Just make tomorrow's schedule today (i.e.,, daily routine should be prepared the day before).

(C) First, write down all the tasks you have tomorrow as you remember them.

(D) Take a good look to see if something has been omitted or if something will go on the cancellation list!

(E) Then divide the tasks into five categories,

    I. Most Important and Urgent. [The tasks which are most important and urgent for you]

    II. Most Important. [The tasks which are most important but not urgent]

    III. Important. [The tasks which are only important for you]

    IV. Delegate. [The tasks you can delegate to other or can outsource]

    V. Eliminate. [The tasks you can eliminate or postpone for the day]

    [You can mark them with A, B, C, D ... for your understanding only]

(F) Give time slots to the most important and urgent tasks first, then arrange them in the order of most important and important.

(G) Then see which tasks you can outsource from the list of tasks or any specific task that is necessary for you but someone else can do it for you. If necessary, you can contact that person and write down the time from him.

(H) Now see if you can eliminate or postpone any tasks from your schedule. If there are any such tasks then you can eliminate or suspend them as you like.

(I) Finally, in this step, sit straight, change your breathing pattern, that is, take a few deep breaths and exhale, after relaxing yourself for a while, and mentally see that you are successfully completing your schedule. In fact, this step will be the mental preparation to overcome your mental obstacles and make the day schedule successful.

Special note; you can allocate some time for your own entertainment. Take small breaks at the end of each task or between tasks and overcome your boredom.

*** Write down any task that you have not been able to complete for some reason and schedule it for the next day.

I will discuss the role of daily schedule more precisely and constructively in the chapter *'Roadmap to Triumph: Unveiling the Steps to Success'*, so you will understand its importance better and you will be able to create a better daily schedule. Instead of waiting for that day, make your day schedule and start fallowing from today.

Along with creating a day schedule and implementing it to its fullest, there are three other very important things to keep in mind if you want to rid your mind of the 'virus' and reprogram your mind. They are Content consume, Choose the People You Spend The Most Time With, and self-talk, all three of which directly and powerfully affect your mind and self-identity.

'It takes a thousand excuses not to do anything, and to do something it takes only the desire of the heart.'

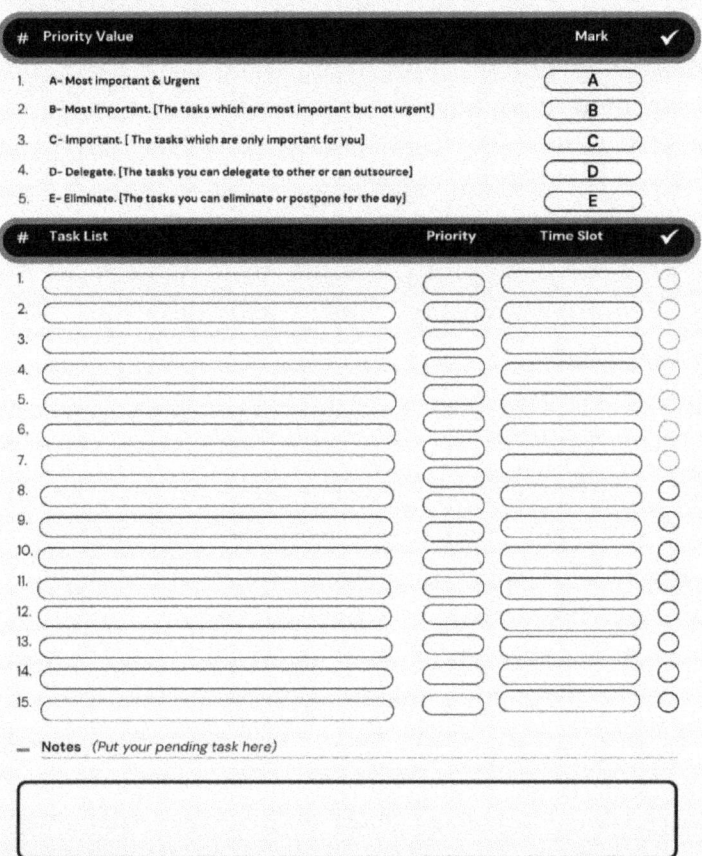

Creating a Positive Media Diet: Curating Content for Mental Health

Now coming to 'Content Consume', because it is a very powerful medium especially in today's era which helps a person to discover his true self and develop a strong mind-set. In today's digital age our minds are constantly bombarded with countless information and content from various sources. All these contents that we consume from various books, articles, podcasts, videos, social media posts, etc., significantly influence our thoughts, beliefs, emotions, feelings and actions. So when all kinds of content are available in front of us cheaply at the touch of a finger we have to be very careful to consume them. Otherwise, we will not even realize when all that content will consume our life, the precious time of life.

You have to increase the ability of 'Deliberate content consume' in a very conscious way. Deliberate content consume is the practice of consciously choosing what to read, watch, and listen to for the purpose of personal growth and self-improvement. This approach goes beyond passive engagement. Though; it requires active selection and critical thinking about content that aligns with one's personal value, goals and aspirations. For example, taking such a holistic approach to reflection and introspection help us better understand our thoughts, emotions, and behaviors. Journals (reading and writing), self-help books, motivational speeches encourage self-reflection. That is, materials that identify our strengths, weaknesses and areas of growth must be chosen. Stories of people who have overcome significant challenges teach us the value of perseverance and tenacity. Narratives like these highlight the importance of embracing failure as a learning opportunity and maintaining a positive outlook even during difficult times. Content related to mental wellness promotes a balanced and focused mind-set. Engagement with such content can increase mental clarity and overall well-being.

Understanding the Impact: Why Your Inner Circle Matters

Motivational speaker Jim Rohn says that *"we are the average of the five people we spend the most time with."* This relates to the law of averages, which is the theory that the result of any given situation will be the average of all outcomes.

Spending most of the day with the right person can profoundly shape your life by boosting your self-image, self-worth and mind-set. The right person provides unwavering support, encouragement and constructive feedback to foster an environment where you can become valued and dilettante. This boost of positive energy helps build your confidence and self-worth, allowing you to see yourself through the lens of potential and ability. By engaging in meaningful conversations and sharing experiences, you can adopt healthy perspectives and attitudes that change the direction of insight. This nurturing dynamic not only inspires you to pursue your goals with greater determination but also instills a deep sense of self-appreciation and belief in your abilities.

Conversely, negative people can drag anyone down by constantly projecting their pessimism and doubt in front of others. Their constant criticism and lack of support can erode your confidence and self-esteem, making you questions your abilities and self-worth. They focus on problems rather than proactive solutions and creating a discouraging environment that stifles creativity and motivation. By highlighting failures and downplaying successes, they can foster feelings of frustration and fear of taking risks. Over time their negative mind-set can lead to stress, anxiety and low self-esteem, which ultimately hinders your personal and professional growth. They can even increase your obstacles many times instead of reducing them. I'm never saying they do all of this intentionally to drag you down, but if you regularly engage in what they do or the discussions they engage in, your subconscious mind will be programmed accordingly.

After knowing everything you have to decide, and choose who you will spend most of your time with.

Transforming Thoughts: How Self-Talk Shapes Your Reality

'Words' have a strange power that can make or destroy people's lives. We can never change the words spoken by others but we can always change our self-talk. We usually talk to ourselves almost all the time when we are awake. Self-dialogue is the internal conversation that is a stream of thoughts and beliefs going through your mind, which can shape your emotions, behavior and ultimately your reality. Self-talk is an important component of mind-set and self-perception that is often underestimated. It can be a powerful tool for personal growth and success when used effectively.

Self-Talk can be classified into two types; Positive and negative. Positive self-talk involves affirming and encouraging thoughts that promote confidence and resilience. On the other hand, negative self-talk is characterized by self-doubt and criticism, which can hinder your progress and well-being.

Think for yourself if an outsider criticizes you, insults you, how much it hurts your heart! And how happy and proud you feel when a person compliments you! But you never notice how many negative words you say to yourself throughout the day, and those are forming your inner world. Negative words about you from outside will hurt you only when you have low self-esteem. If your self-identity is clear to yourself, it will not affect what other says or does.

Effects of self-talk on Mind-Set:

Positive self-talk fuels a growth mind-set by reinforcing the belief that challenges are opportunities to learn. Statements like "I can improve myself with practice" or "Every setback is a setup for a comeback" encourage persistence and adaptability.

Conversely negative self-talk creates a fixed mind-set. Phrases like "I'm not good enough", "I'll never succeed", "God gave me all the trouble", or "I'm just unlucky" create mental barriers that prevent you from taking risks and exploring your full potential.

Role of self-talk in self-perception:

Indeed self-realization is the process of understanding and fulfilling potential. It recognizes your strengths, weaknesses and inherent values. Self-talk is helpful in this journey, as it will either clarify or obscure your self-concept. Positive self-talk helps you acknowledge your accomplishments, qualities and potential. It encourages self-compassion and a realistic assessment of your abilities, which are essential to overcoming obstacles and setting meaningful goals.

Conversely, negative self-talk can distort your self-image, leading to self-doubt and diminished self-worth. This can create a cycle of negativity that blinds you to your strengths and potential.

Strategies for Transforming Self-Talk:

Awareness and Observation: - The first step in transforming self-talk is awareness of it. Pay attention to your inner dialogue and identify negative thinking patterns, documenting everything if necessary, because until you are well aware of when, under what circumstances and what negative self-talk is going within you, you cannot easily change it.

Challenge Negative Thoughts: - Once you identify negative self-talk, challenge its validity. Ask yourself if you even have evidence to support these thoughts or if they are just based on your assumptions and fears of the current situation. Ask yourself what arguments you have against what you say about yourself. Then replace negative statements with specific positive realistic affirmations.

Reframing: - Reframing involves changing your perspective on a situation. Don't see a mistake as a failure; see it as a learning opportunity. This shift in perspective can significantly change your self-talk and mind-set. At the same time, be grateful to yourself and others. At least learn to be grateful to yourself for the storm that you are enduring and moving forward! Acknowledging and praising your strengths and accomplishments regularly will encourage positive self-talk.

Affirmation: - Affirmation is to firmly establish oneself or one's statement. Self-affirmations are positive phrases or statements used to challenge any barriers created by our negative thoughts. And if this method is repeated again and again it becomes our belief. I know of no better tool than self-affirmation to motivate yourself, change your mind-set by improving your self-image, and increase your worth. Affirmation is a very powerful tool for changing mind-sets and fulfilling your desires.

Affirmation Technique:

I would always suggest that you practice affirmation in such a way that it becomes your inner dialogue and I never advocate that you have to follow any specific rules i.e.,, affirmation should be done at night or in the morning. Start by shouting or affirming to yourself as often as you like throughout the day or night if you can. Don't stop doing affirmations until they connect with your inner feelings and become inner dialogue. But while doing this the steps that must be taken into consideration are mentioned below-

- **Identify what you desire: -** Identify your desires very specifically, what you really want to get or what you want to be - be it health, wealth, life, relationships, personal growth, whatever it may be.
- **Positive Framing: -** Phrase your shots positively. Instead of saying "I don't want to be stressed" use "I am calm and

relaxed". Focus on what you want, not what you don't want. Use words that trigger strong and positive emotions.

- **Frame your affirmations in the present tense:** - Frame your affirmations in the present tense as if they are happening in your life right now. For example "I am confident and successful".
- **Keep them short and simple:** - The simpler and shorter the affirmation, the easier it will be to remember and repeat it. Long broad statements have more complexity and less power.
- **Consistency is key:** - Repeat those multiple times daily. The more you repeat them, the faster they will be embedded in your subconscious mind.
- **Feel the emotions:** - Feel the emotions associated with your affirmation. If you make an affirmation about success, try to feel it, visualize what it looks like!

Remember that the keys to effective affirmations are repetition with belief and emotional engagement. By practicing this powerful tool consistently and with conviction you can reprogram your subconscious mind to support your wishes and desires.

Conclusion:

In conclusion, the chapter emphasizes the critical role of mindfulness in managing mental influences in today's digital age. By recognizing and combating mind viruses through conscious content consumption, structured scheduling, and positive self-talk, individuals can enhance their mental resilience and productivity. Implementing these strategies empowers individuals to reclaim control over their minds, fostering an environment conducive to personal growth and success. By applying these principles consistently, individuals can navigate challenges more effectively and cultivate a mind-set that promotes lifelong learning and achievement.

CHAPTER 5

Roadmap to Triumph: Unveiling the Steps to Success

Don't underestimate your capabilities

Success is a reflection of one's capabilities honed through dedication and learning from experiences. It emerges when individuals harness their strengths and navigate obstacles with strategic thinking and adaptability. Each achievement underscores the potential within, fueling a cycle of continuous improvement and innovation. Recognizing and leveraging these capabilities fosters a path where goals are not just met, but exceeded, shaping a legacy of impactful contributions and lasting influence.

'Within your subconscious mind lies a myriad of keys to unlock the doors of success along the path of your journey.'

The word success itself is a beacon of aspiration, an exciting concept that drives countless endeavours and inspires the dreams of individuals worldwide. But what exactly is success? This chapter explores the multifaceted nature of success, uncovering its complexities and uncovering its true essence.

In the traditional view, success is often measured by tangible achievements, wealth, status, and power. This traditional view sees success as a destination, a point to be reached that is often validated by external and social standards.

Consider the stories of moguls like Andrew Carnegie and John Davison Rockefeller, whose success was marked by great fortune and influence. Yet in reality the narratives paint a picture of success as a prize won through hard work, strategy, and sometimes ruthless determination.

A personal measure or dimension of success can never be the same; success is not a ONE-SIZE-FITS concept. What one person sees as the pinnacle of achievement may be of little value to another. In fact success is deeply personal, with individual values that are shaped by goals and passions. Imagine two artists, the first measuring success by his ability to create and express, finding fulfilment in the act of creation rather than public acclaim or monetary rewards. Success for him can be a quiet, intimate satisfaction that follows his craft with authenticity and passion. On the contrary, the measure of success for the second person is how much popularity he gained, how much money he earned, public appreciation etc.

To fully grasp the essence of success we must define failure. Failure is seen as the opposite of proactive success, a sign of inadequacy or defeat. However, failure is an integral part of describing success. It is through failure that we learn, adapt, and ultimately become stronger. The story of Thomas Edison is proof of this. His numerous failed attempts to create the electric light bulb were not seen as setbacks. Rather it was seen as a necessary step towards its ultimate success. Edison famously remarked, ***"I haven't failed; I've just found ten thousand ways that won't work."***

Defining Success: Understanding What It Truly Means

The first and most important thing to know in order to be successful is to have a clear idea of what success is and what it means. When I ask participants in my Mental Wellness Mastery Program what success means, some say becoming a billionaire, some say getting a job, some say becoming a big sportsman, and some say becoming famous, that is, no specific answer is available, everyone gives opinions according to everyone's perception. I understand how much they actually lack ideas about success. But to achieve success it is necessary to have a clear idea about it.

Analyzing everything that many people have said about success, I realized that "success is the progressive realization of worthy ideas". Here 'worthy ideas' are those that are life-cantered and will make life better. A person who has a worthy idea and continues to work on that idea for his own growth is a real success. Success cannot be limited to achieving any specific goal. It is not limited to material gain or external validation; it is a dynamically evolving journey rather than a fixed destination. But that certainly does not mean that it is a purposeless journey. Purposeless life is a nomadic life. It is a method through which continuous growth is possible. The even more bitter truth is that success is never the absence of problems; on the contrary, success is a way of making yourself stronger so that you become more courageous to face problems. Success is multifaceted; it includes concepts of personal growth, meaningful relationships, happiness, purpose, and fulfilment. Take my example. Before starting this book, my goal was to write a book, and my great intention was that the book would give a clear path to millions of people like you to get rid of their life problems and lead a happy, prosperous, and successful life. And who has benefited the most when I have been working towards that goal? Myself! Because I have gained so much experience and knowledge while writing this book, I have grown many times over.

To give you a deeper understanding of success, I have shared a beautiful moral story with you.

There was a small forest next to a remote village in Africa. There was a banyan tree and a bamboo tree among the different trees in that forest. They have just begun to break through the ground. Barely in the glory of the forest have they grown slowly with purpose, as time goes on and they also grow, but in the law of nature the bamboo grows rapidly and becomes much taller than the banyan tree.

One day the bamboo tree looked at the stem of the banyan tree and said "Look at me; I am the tallest in the forest' not only you, no one else in this forest can touch me, I have reached the pinnacle of success; my success is obvious to everyone. On the other hand, you are very small and weak. What do you hope to achieve?"

The banyan tree listened quietly but did not answer. It slowly grows inch by inch, day by day - nurtured by rain and sun. Years passed, and the bamboo tree was very proud and arrogant. Meanwhile, the banyan tree grew quite tall and strong, its branches also spread quite wide and provided shelter for innumerable animals.

One day, a strong storm blew through the forest. The wind howled, and the torrential downpour began. The bamboo tree, which was proud of its success, was swayed by the storm and fell down with its roots. Although a few branches of the banyan tree were broken by the strong storm, but finally when the storm stopped the banyan tree stood tall. He has managed to protect the animals in his shelter. He has succeeded in his great purpose.

The strong banyan then spoke softly to the bamboo: "Dear bamboo, you were really tall, your head was sky high. But true success is not just about being tall, it's about resilience, adaptability, growth and contribution. I may have started with slow steps, but I managed to drive my roots deep, I strengthened myself, I learned to bend with obstacles, I learned to face challenges, I deep rooted myself to face challenges, and I learned to grow steadily. My success lies not only in my height but in my ability to withstand life's ups and downs and grow."

The fallen bamboo tree reflected on the banyan tree's words and realized that he only cared about being tall - never thinking about getting himself deeply rooted which could help him face all the challenges. He realized that success is not just about showing off or competition; it's about enduring hardship, learning from failure and growing with each experience. It is actually a journey of what you want to serve the greater purpose that develops through continuous growth and self-improvement.

The story of the banyan tree and the bamboo tree imparts profound lessons about success, and the true meaning of growth and contribution.

Initially, the bamboo tree grows rapidly, towering over its surroundings and proclaiming itself as the tallest and most successful in the forest. Its success seems obvious and unquestionable. In contrast, the banyan tree grows slowly and steadily, silently observing the bamboo's boastfulness but focusing on its own growth and contribution.

As time passes, a severe storm tests the strength of both trees. Despite its height, the bamboo tree, lacking deep roots and flexibility, succumbs to the storm and falls. On the other hand, though the banyan tree suffers some damage, it ultimately remains standing, having weathered the storm due to its deep roots and ability to bend without breaking.

The banyan tree then imparts a gentle but powerful lesson to the fallen bamboo tree. It explains that true success is not merely about outward achievements or height, but about resilience, adaptability, and the ability to endure and grow through challenges. The banyan tree's success lies not only in its physical stature but also in its capacity to provide shelter and support to others, symbolizing a deeper purpose and contribution to the forest ecosystem.

The fallen bamboo tree learns that its focus on rapid growth and outward success overlooked the importance of building a strong foundation and developing resilience. It reflects on how true success involves continuous growth, learning from failures, and becoming deeply rooted in values and strengths that withstand adversity.

Ultimately, the story teaches us several key lessons:

1. **Resilience and Adaptability:** Success is not just about achieving some goals but about enduring setbacks, adapting to challenges, and bouncing back stronger.
2. **Continuous Growth:** True success involves on going personal and professional development, learning from experiences, and evolving over time. Success isn't a destination but a journey of constant growth and evolution.
3. **Purpose and Contribution:** Success is meaningful when it serves a greater purpose, such as providing support to others or contributing positively to the community or for universe. Without a greater purpose, success loses its depth and significance. It is the alignment of our achievements with meaningful goals that gives purpose to our journey, enriching our lives and impacting the world around us.
4. **Deep Rootedness:** Building a strong foundation, both personally and professionally, ensures sustainability and the ability to withstand life's storms.

In essence, the story encourages us to look beyond superficial measures of success and focus on qualities like resilience, adaptability, and continuous growth that lead to enduring fulfilment and positive impact in the world.

That day, my traveling companion was a twenty-two-year-old freshman, and we engaged in a delightful conversation during our long journey. The boy's youthful energy was palpable, and his positive body language spoke volumes about his vibrant personality. Given my background in mind Science, I find joy in conversing with people of all ages, professions, and backgrounds.

I have a knack for building rapport easily; genuine interest in others allows me to forge strong friendships effortlessly. I listen attentively, seeking to understand others openly and sincerely, without any hint of insincerity.

I struck up a strong friendship with the boy. He excelled academically, achieving excellent marks in secondary school, higher secondary, and throughout his graduation. Curious about his future plans, I asked him what his goals were now that he had completed his studies. The boy, who had been open and confident in our conversations thus far, seemed momentarily caught off guard by my question. After a pause, he replied somewhat hesitantly, "I'm thinking of pursuing higher education and also preparing for various competitive exams. If I manage to secure a government job, then I'll consider myself successful. After that, I'll stop studying and start working."

As he continued, expressing concern about the current job market, "Look at the situation now. No matter how diligently you study or how well you perform, good opportunities are scarce. Talented individuals, both young men and women, are losing hope due to the lack of job openings in both the public and private sectors."

As he expressed these concerns, I interjected gently, pausing his train of thought. I posed a direct question: "What is your ultimate goal in life? What do you aspire to become?"

The boy responded promptly, "I wanted to become a college principal, but what else can I do? There are hardly any jobs available! And even if there are, opportunities are often given to less qualified candidates through bribery. Despite achieving good results, I fear I won't get a fair chance. So, realistically, if I manage to secure a clerical position or any Group D job, at least life would be somewhat assured."

As he spoke, a hint of despair shadowed his face, causing the brightness in his eyes and expression to dim. It was a natural response, faced with the stark reality where newspaper headlines regularly highlight grim truths like "unemployment numbers on the rise" and "candidates securing jobs despite submitting blank answer sheets, including B.Tech and M.Tech graduates applying for Group 'D' positions."

Certainly, it's undeniable that the current situation may be challenging. However, let me pose a question: 'Despite these challenges, are not being recruited? Are young people not pursuing their dream careers? Are people not finding their path to success?'

Undoubtedly, progress may vary, but take a closer look around you—regardless of your field of interest or study, there are individuals achieving notable success. Why can't you be among them? You have the potential to achieve similar success if you're willing to learn, understand, and emulate the strategies of successful people in your chosen field.

Success is not unattainable if you study the paths taken by successful individuals—observe their actions, their mind-set, their dedication, and their strategies for success. Emulate their approach, adapt it to your circumstances, and commit yourself wholeheartedly. With determination and perseverance, you can undoubtedly achieve comparable success in your own journey.

When we look at successful individuals, their standard of living and lifestyle captivate us. We observe their clothing, cars, homes, dining habits, and their renown. However, we seldom delve into their life stories before their success, nor do we often attempt to emulate or learn from their journeys.

However, there is a psychological reasoning behind this phenomenon. The science of the mind suggests that our psyche inherently seeks pleasure while avoiding pain. The challenges, obstacles, and adversities that every successful person encounters on their path to success are often overlooked because our minds instinctively recoil from the potential discomfort they might entail. Instead, people are naturally drawn to the allure of enjoying the fruits of success.

It's never like you're enjoying your life or your life is smooth sailing by not taking on the challenges you need to be successful, avoiding obstacles and pain! Everything is happening in your life too, you have pain, you have challenges in life, but only you have become accustomed to them and become intimate with it, and so avoiding new pain for a few months or years is inviting disaster for the rest of your life. While avoiding temporary pain, you are preventing yourself from enjoying the happiness of success throughout your life.

That 22-year-old freshman may have worked hard throughout his life, yet he has never dedicated time to discovering his life's goals and purpose through brainstorming. He does not know what his real goal is; let alone his purpose and vision. One can never go far without a clear goal. Even with his talent, he may settle for a job that may not satisfy him. However, if he starts finding his purpose and goal in life from now on, he will definitely be able to achieve great success at a young age because he will be able to take action with full focus.

I will tell a remarkable real-life story and then return to our main topic. You might already be familiar with this story, as it is about the legendary Sachin Tendulkar, often referred to as the God of Cricket. (Although the story is collected.)

The game was unfolding in Sharjah, and Sachin played brilliantly throughout the series. It can be said that this series was one of the best tournaments of his life. After winning the final match, the entire team celebrated their victory with great joy. In this match, Sachin was likely the man of the match, and he was also named the man of the tournament. The Indian team was elated, and a party was arranged to last the entire night.

However, the centre of the team's joy, Sachin Tendulkar, took a plane at two in the morning straight to Mumbai. When he arrived, it was around 4 or 4:30 a.m. Instead of going home, he went directly to Wankhede Stadium. After about four hours of practice, he finally returned home. When he entered the stadium, the young cricketers and their coaches were astonished to see him. The man who had performed so exceptionally well the previous night, bringing immense joy to all of India, had travelled by air overnight and chosen to practice on the field rather than going home!

Sachin did not become the God of Cricket by chance. He was not elevated to this status by the audience, social media, or news media promotion. People accepted him as the God of Cricket because of his relentless work ethic towards his greater purpose, indomitable willpower, and unwavering dedication to cricket.

I briefly shared this story with you because I want to make you understand that behind every success lies a deep commitment—a commitment to dedicate oneself, often at the expense of many small and large interests. When Sachin practiced by returning from Sharjah early in the morning, he had already established himself as one of the best cricketers in the world. Missing practice for two or five days likely wouldn't have affected his career. Sachin could have enjoyed a late-night party and returned home the next day, or he could have gone straight home from the airport to enjoy the comfort of his own space.

However, Sachin's devotion to cricket is so profound that it is his passion, his source of joy, and the essence of his life. Cricket is his dharma, his karma, and everything he stands for. This unwavering commitment is what sets him apart and serves as a powerful lesson in dedication and love for one's craft.

In my training and coaching sessions, I make it a point to inquire about each participant's primary goal and purpose in life. Sadly, the responses reveal a stark reality: only small fractions, approximately one to two percent, are able to articulate their aspirations clearly and directly. The vast majority appear uncertain, struggling to articulate coherent answers that truly reflect their ambitions or life's purpose. For many, the future remains shrouded in ambiguity, leaving them unsure about their next steps!

It is truly unfortunate when individuals—be they young; B.Tech. engineers, recent graduates, or even those over fifty—find themselves uncertain about their life's purpose and direction. Without a clear understanding of their purpose, how can they begin their journey or hope to reach a meaningful destination? Starting a journey without a defined goal is akin to wandering aimlessly; one risks becoming lost in the crowd, settling for any path that presents itself.

Everyone possesses immense potential, yet without a clear sense of purpose, many drift along with the prevailing currents of societal expectations or personal uncertainty. This predicament cannot be solely attributed to youth; numerous factors, such as familial pressures or a lack of guidance, contribute to this state of indecision.

However, sitting idle guarantees stagnation rather than success. The key to progress lies in initiating the journey towards success promptly. Crucially, this journey begins with a lucid vision of one's destination—setting clear, achievable goals. Before delving into specific goal-setting methodologies, it is vital to acknowledge and relinquish whatever impedes our path to success.

Essential Give up: Key Steps to Achieve Extraordinary Success

DON'T PLAY BLAME GAME:

The blame game is a perilous cycle that ensnares you, hindering your progress and thwarting your path to true success. It's a trap that many of us unwittingly fall into, whether in your personal lives or professional endeavours. Continuously pointing fingers keeps us mired in negativity and unproductivity, stunting our growth.

It's crucial to break free from this cycle. Blaming external factors may provide temporary relief or justification, but it does nothing to alter your current circumstances. Saying things like "I couldn't invest in my business because the bank refused my loan, leading to losses," or "My advancement was blocked by my superiors," might seem valid from your perspective, but such accusations do not empower you to change your situation.

True success demands accountability and a proactive approach. Instead of dwelling on what went wrong or who might be at fault, focus on what you can control and how you can move forward constructively. By taking ownership of your actions and decisions, you reclaim the power to shape your own destiny. This shift in mind-set is pivotal to breaking free from the blame trap and paving the way for genuine success.

Embrace Accountability:

The main reason the 'blame game' hinders our success is because it creates the illusion of control. When we blame others or external circumstances for failure, we feel a temporary sense of relief. By avoiding taking responsibility, we believe that the situation will naturally change, back in our favor. This sense of control is deceptive and fleeting. In fact, by blaming others, we surrender our energy to change and improve ourselves.

Stagnation and Victim Mentality:

Blaming others often leads to stagnation and a victim mentality. Instead of taking proactive steps to meet challenges and achieve success, we get stuck in a cycle of self-pity and pointing fingers. We convince ourselves that only external factors are responsible for our misfortunes. Instead of acknowledging our situation we just wait and get frustrated. This victim mentality inhibits the development of personal growth, innovation, and resilience—qualities that are essential to achieving success.

Loss of relationship:

Engaging in the blame game can have dire consequences for our relationships, both personally and professionally. Constantly blaming others creates a toxic environment of distrust and hostility. It erodes the foundation for cooperation and teamwork, hinders progress, and inhibits creative problem solving. When blame becomes the norm, people may avoid taking risks on your behalf, fearing the consequences of failure and subsequent blame.

Shifting focus from solutions to more problems:

Blaming others keeps us stuck in the problem instead of finding a solution, not wanting to shift our focus from there. When we fixate on finding fault with others, we neglect to analyze the root causes of the problems we face. Instead of thinking about innovative ideas and taking action, we get stuck in a negative cycle of endless blaming. This fixation prevents us from learning from mistakes, adapting to change and ultimately finding success.

How to get rid of the blame game?

Let's see how to get rid of the blame game-

Embrace Accountability:

We must develop a mind-set of accountability to move beyond the blame game. Acknowledge your role in both success and failure. Recognize that external factors can affect outcomes, but you have control over your own actions and reactions. By taking responsibility ensure that you are ready to empower yourself to make positive changes and take steps towards success.

Shift the focus from blame to learning:

Instead of pointing fingers, reframe your mind-set to focus on learning. When faced with obstacles, see them as opportunities for growth and improvement. Analyze the situation objectively, try to understand what went wrong, and prepare for how you can prevent similar challenges in the future. This shift in perspective will equip you with new knowledge and insight to help you move forward.

Open yourself up to communication:

Success is rarely achieved alone, so cooperation and support can greatly accelerate the pace of success. Cultivate a culture of cooperation and support in your personal and professional relationships. Encourage open communication so that others feel safe to share their ideas and concerns without holding back for fear of blaming. Emphasize the importance of collective problem solving, focusing on finding solutions rather than focusing on mistakes.

Develop a growth mind-set:

Develop a growth mind-set - a belief that skills, intelligence can be developed through dedication and hard work. Embrace challenges as opportunities to learn and improve. Celebrate everything you learn and experience along the way. By adopting a growth mind-set you can free yourself from the limitations of blame and a world of possibilities can open up to you.

Remember that ***success is within your reach when you stop blaming and take ownership of your journey.***

Abandoning ego:

A powerful obstacle that often stands in our way in our pursuit of success is our own ego. The ego's voice within us, who craves validation and control, can hinder our progress and stifle our ability to achieve true success. In this topic, we will explore how the ego holds us back, the extent of its influence in our lives, and learn effective strategies for overcoming its influence.

The ego, in a nutshell, is your sense of self – your unique identity made up of thoughts, feelings, experiences, and beliefs. It acts as a mediator between your inner world (desires, instincts) and the outer world (perceived reality, social norms).

This broader view focuses on the ego as the conscious "I" that shapes how you perceive yourself and the world. Your ego develops through your experiences and interactions with others. As you grow, your sense of self refines based on:

- **Social interactions:** How others see you and respond to you.
- **Accomplishments and failures:** These experiences shape your self-esteem and confidence.
- **Values and beliefs:** The ideas you internalize become part of your self-concept.

Nature of 'Ego':

Before we deal with the problem of the ego, it is essential to understand its nature. The sense of ego is never inherently negative; it is an integral part of our human psyche. It is that voice within us that wants to protect our projected-selves. However, if not taken seriously and properly examined, the ego can become an obstacle that can block growth and success.

Effect of Ego on Success:

Ego exerts a profound influence on our journey toward success, impacting us in several critical ways.

Ego initially blinds us to our weaknesses, obstructing our ability to acknowledge areas needing improvement. This lack of self-awareness becomes a barrier to both personal and professional growth. As we experience small successes, our ego can inflate, shifting our focus away from personal development towards self-indulgence. This diversion often leads to significant setbacks in life.

Additionally, ego magnifies the fear of failure, discouraging us from taking risks and exploring new opportunities. It confines us within our comfort zone, limiting our potential for growth and innovation.

How will you overcome this obstacle?

Building Self Awareness:

To overcome the ego's grip on us, we must first develop self-awareness. By developing a deeper understanding of ourselves we need to identify the moments when ego arises. Mental wellness practices and positive mental health practices help us observe our thoughts, emotions and reactions. This awareness allows us to detach from our egoic mind that dictates and make conscious choices that align with our true goals. The more you discover your true self, the fewer egos remain.

Embracing 'Humility':

'Humility' - acts as a powerful antidote to ego. By acknowledging our limitations and embracing 'humility', we can open ourselves up to continuous learning and growth. Embracing humility involves valuing the perspectives and contributions of others. It recognizes that success is a collaborative effort. It certainly teaches us to learn from mistakes, ask for feedback from others when needed, and admit that we don't have all the answers.

Focusing on process:

Egoism focuses on external validation and results which often overshadows the value of the journey. To break free from this trap, we must shift our focus from the external measures of success to the process of growth and self-improvement. By setting intrinsic goals and celebrating small milestones we can find fulfilment in the progress we make each day.

Practicing empathy and connection:

Ego develops in the division between 'I' and 'YOU'. To overcome its rigidity, you must become empathetic and develop connections with others. By building genuine relationships, actively listening, and trying to understand different perspectives, you can break down the ego and break free of the barriers it creates. Cooperating and supporting others not only benefits them but enhances your own growth and success.

Ego is a powerful adversary on the path to success, but with self-awareness, humility and focusing on growth, you can overcome its negative influence. By recognizing the ways in which the ego hinders your progress, you can make a conscious effort to silence its voice and embrace a mind-set that encourages collaboration, continuous learning, and personal growth. Only by overcoming your ego you can unleash your full potential and accelerate your way to success in life.

Eliminating Excuses

In other words, the third hand of man is "excuse," which is much longer than the other two hands. When people lose faith in themselves, when they think there's nothing else to do, or when they want to avoid something, they build a wall of excuses. Most of the time, people don't understand that these walls are not meant to stop others or block obstacles but are meant to block their own growth and invite failure. Excuses, whether given to oneself or others, must have an effect. Sometime you may understand the direct effect, but the indirect impact of making excuses can be even more profound.

Excuses are the weapons people use to avoid their responsibilities and keep them in a safe and comfortable position.

However, if we think long-term, we can understand how badly this impacts our lives. It is true that responsibility can be avoided temporarily with excuses, but that responsibility will one day become a huge burden on our shoulders. The safe and comfortable position we try to put ourselves in with excuses is actually a well-furnished bed of thorns for our future. Saying, "I don't have enough time" may allow you to avoid something momentarily, but it gives massage to your subconscious mind that making excuses is safe for you. Later, during critical moments, your subconscious mind might generate excuses that could cause you to miss valuable opportunities. If you say, "I will do it tomorrow," it signals to your mind that you are a master of procrastination, making it difficult to break that habit. People are adept at coming up with numerous excuses such as:

- Time-related Excuses:
    - "I'll do it tomorrow."
    - "I'm too busy right now."
- Capability-related Excuses:
    - "I'm not good enough."
    - "I don't have the skills."
    - "I'm not smart enough."
- Circumstance-related Excuses:
    - "It's not the right time."
    - "Things are too complicated right now."
    - "I have too many other responsibilities."
- Fear-based Excuses:
    - "I might fail."
    - "What if people judge me?"
    - "I'm afraid of what might happen."

- Health-related Excuses:
    - "I'm too tired."
    - "I don't feel well."
    - "I need to rest."
- Resource-related Excuses:
    - "I don't have enough money."
    - "I don't have the right tools or equipment."
    - "I don't have enough support."
- Motivation-related Excuses:
    - "I'm not motivated enough."
    - "I don't feel like it."
    - "I'm not in the mood."
- External Blame Excuses:
    - "It's someone else's fault."
    - "The situation is out of my control."
    - "If only I had more help."
- Comparison-based Excuses:
    - "Others are better at this."
    - "No one else is doing it."
    - "It's easier for them."
- Perfectionism Excuses:
    - "It's not perfect yet."
    - "I need more time to make it better."
    - "I'll start when everything is perfect."

People can make thousands of such excuses to temporarily avoid responsibility or make themselves feel safe and comfortable. However, if you want to move towards success and fulfil a greater purpose, you must bury all the excuses.

Recently, I came across a video on social media of a lady doing gym exercises with her two to three-month-old baby on her lap. She was doing push-ups, pull-ups, and bicep exercises with the baby in her arms. Despite having a thousand reasons not to go to the gym, she found a way. In contrast, many people make New Year's resolutions to keep their bodies healthy on January 1st, by joining the gym. But as soon as the week goes by, they start making excuses: "I am not feeling well today," "It is raining," or "I didn't wake up today." Think about it— who is actually harmed by giving these excuses? Yes, in some cases, there may be genuine reasons for not taking immediate action, but in most cases, excuses make small reasons appear to be bigger problems and actually encourage us not to take action.

Every excuse you make is a justification for avoiding action, a rationalization for staying within your comfort zones. When you allow excuses to dictate your decisions, you forfeit the chance to evolve and improve yourself. Excuses become a shield against discomfort and a hindrance to growth. Giving excuses can be one of the greatest obstacles in human life for achieving success because it cultivates a mind-set of avoidance rather than accountability. When you make excuses, you shift the blame away from yourself and onto external factors, diminishing your sense of control and responsibility over your own actions and outcomes. This habit can lead to a pattern of inaction and complacency, where opportunities are missed, and growth is stunted.

Excuses can create a barrier to self-improvement, as they prevent you from recognizing and addressing your weaknesses. By refusing to acknowledge your shortcomings, you deny yourself the chance to learn from your mistakes and to develop the resilience needed to overcome challenges. This lack of personal growth can result in a stagnation of skills and abilities, making it harder to achieve your goals.

Moreover, consistently giving excuses can erode trust and credibility with others. In professional and personal relationships, reliability and accountability are highly valued. If we are known for making excuses, people may perceive us as unreliable or uncommitted, which can limit opportunities for collaboration, mentorship, and advancement.

Ultimately, success requires a proactive approach to life's challenges. It involves taking ownership of your actions, learning from failures, and continually striving for improvement. By eliminating excuses, you empower yourself to take control of your destiny, face obstacles head-on, and achieve your fullest potential.

HOW TO STOP MAKING EXCUSES

Making excuses is normal from time to time – we're all humans, after all. But if it's starting to interfere with your life and prevent you from reaching your goals, it's time to learn how to stop making excuses. Here's how:

How to stop making excuses:

➤ You need a big 'WHY' to stop making excuses:

When you have a crystal clear picture inside your mind about what you are doing and why you are doing it, you will never try to make excuses. That's why I say *you need a thousand excuses not to do something but one big reason is enough to do it.* So find out why you should do the things you usually make excuses for, and what will you achieve in the future by doing this!

➤ Identify what safety or comfort you want to maintain by making excuses:

To avoid making excuses, it's important to know what security or comfort you're actually making excuses for. And after knowing this, ask yourself whether that safe or comfortable position is really safe or comfortable for you, or is going to cause danger in the future!

> *Identify what fears your excuses are expressing:*

In all cases where you are making excuses out of fear, be sure to ask yourself –

"What am I afraid of?"

"How realistic is this fear?"

"What might happen if I do the deed?"

> *Taking Responsibility*

I have elaborated extensively on the concept of taking responsibility; you can delve into it for a comprehensive understanding. It is crucial to recognize that the path to shaping your future lies solely in assuming responsibility. Excuses cannot absolve you of this responsibility, for your life is entirely your own. Embracing responsibility is the key to transforming challenges into opportunities. Therefore, you have a choice: take responsibility and catalyze change in your life, or persist in making excuses.

Furthermore, overcoming the habit of making excuses necessitates clear goal-setting and a well-defined sense of purpose and vision, topics which I will delve into extensively in the next discussion.

Strategic Goal Setting: Your Blueprint for Success

Even the youngest among us understand the importance of setting goals to achieve success! Yet, how many of us truly set goals, align ourselves with them, stay committed, and consistently put in the effort required?

Superficially setting a goal may spark initial enthusiasm, but without inner motivation, it fizzles out quickly. Even with abundant opportunities, achieving that goal becomes elusive. True success never comes without crystal-clear objectives. I like to think of goals as life's outcomes—what we aim to achieve should be nothing short of 'PERFECT'. Just as the word 'PERFECT' implies flawlessness, our goals must be perfectly suited to us. Each letter in 'PERFECT' forms a powerful framework for setting life goals. If your goals are aligned with this formula, they become not just acceptable but achievable.

In the pursuit of our ambitions, setting clear and strategic goals is crucial for making meaningful progress. Whether it is personal growth, career advancement, or fulfilling lifelong dreams, goal setting provides us with direction, motivation, and a structured path to success.

This chapter explores the art and science of strategic goal setting, highlighting its pivotal role in turning aspirations into concrete accomplishments. By learning how to define objectives effectively, align them with our broader vision, and take actionable steps, we empower ourselves to navigate challenges, discover opportunities, and ultimately unlock our full potential.

The 'PERFECT' goal-setting formula not only clarifies our priorities but also fosters a mind-set of accountability and perseverance. This systematic approach encourages us to envision our desired future and take intentional steps towards its realization. As we embark on this journey together, let's delve into the principles and practices that will enable you to create your personal blueprint for success through strategic application of the 'PERFECT' goal-setting methodology.

DEEP SENSE OF PURPOSE:

'Steer your emotions with purpose, for they hold the power to drive you towards greatness.'

The first letter 'P' in 'PERFECT' signifies purposes—the fundamental reason for existence. When your purpose and goals are not aligned, when there is discord between them, true congruence becomes elusive. The search for purpose is one of life's deepest quests, as it imbues our lives with meaning and provides direction. Like a steadfast North Star, purpose guides us through challenges and towards victories alike. It is the cornerstone that harmonizes our aspirations with our ultimate reason for being.

Behind every remarkable success lies a profound purpose. Observing highly successful individuals reveals a common thread—they are driven by or dedicated to a higher purpose. Purpose is the antidote to aimlessness; losing sight of it means wandering without direction or clarity in our pursuits. Therefore, discovering your purpose is paramount.

If you struggle to define your purpose, remember that sometimes your life's purpose is to imbue life itself with purpose.

It's about uncovering why you exist in this vast universe. Understanding this core question unveils your greater calling, resonating with your passions, strengths, values, and sources of fulfilment.

Your life's purpose is something that fuels tireless dedication. It sustains you through long hours of focused work without fatigue, hunger, or boredom. External accolades or rewards become secondary; intrinsic motivation drives your efforts consistently. This inner drive ensures enduring enthusiasm and unwavering commitment to your chosen path.

Many authors advocate discovering your strengths and talents as a starting point for finding purpose—identifying what you excel in and where your natural abilities lie. However, I hold a different perspective on this matter. I firmly believe that one can cultivate strength and proficiency in any area, regardless of initial competence. A prime example is Mahendra Singh Dhoni, who began his journey as a skilled football goalkeeper. Despite his prowess in football, he redirected his focus upon discovering his life's purpose, transitioning to cricket. Through relentless dedication, he emerged not only as a formidable cricketer but also as a transformative captain and wicketkeeper-batsman for the Indian national team, leaving an indelible mark on the sport.

In my view, identifying purpose does not hinge on existing strengths or talents. Instead, it begins with crystallizing a vivid vision in your mind.

Vision: Your vision paints a picture of the world as you wish to see it—the ideal environment where you find true happiness. It defines what a beautiful world means to you and serves as your guiding light.

For instance, my vision is, *'I want to build such a society, such a world where the success of people with good intentions will eradicate the bad intentions of people. I want to build a good humanistic world for the next generation'*. This statement encapsulates how I envision the world and steers my actions towards achieving this goal. This book is an integral part of my journey in that direction.

Personally, once I discovered my vision, mission, and purpose in life, my perspective shifted from dwelling on limitations and grievances to pursuing growth and making meaningful contributions. Today, external validation or criticism holds little sway over me compared to the fulfilment derived from aligning with my mission and vision. If ever a day passes without advancing towards my mission and vision, it leaves me with a profound sense of regret.

Finding vision and purpose transcends initial capabilities; it is about envisioning a better world and taking intentional steps towards making it a reality.

In fact, vision is much more than just a goal or ambition. This is an aspirational picture of what you want to achieve, who you want to be, and what kind of world that picture will reflect. Vision looks beyond immediate concerns to the future, painting a vivid and inspiring picture that evokes indomitable willpower. In contrast to goals, which are often specific and time-bound, vision is broad and encompassing, acting as a beacon that illuminates the way forward. This becomes significantly easier when we have a clear vision. A well-defined vision provides clarity about where you want to go. This clarity can help you understand what is important to you in the sense of affirmation, expressing your values and emotions that are integral to your purpose.

So it is one of the most important and urgent tests. Find your vision, and to do this, ask yourself:

- What is my core value in life?
- What are the things I am passionate about?
- What impact do I want to make on the world?
- If it were my dream world, what would it look like?

- What is the most valuable thing that I will never get bored or get tired of doing?
- What legacy do I want to leave behind?

Sure, it's brainstorming, but once you do it, you'll gain a lot of clarity about life and about yourself. Sit down with a pen and notepad to answer each question mentioned above. Write thoughtful answers to each question. You may not get clarity at first, but write again and again and try to understand.

Once you have a clear picture of your vision, you can easily set your goals, and your mission will be clear in your subconscious mind.

Mission: The mission is what steps you will take to fulfil your vision and what you will do to achieve your life's purpose! Imagine if your vision is to create a world where green landscapes thrive with clean, fresh air, and minimal pollution. What would your mission be in such a scenario? Perhaps it involves planting millions of trees, nurturing them, encouraging others to join in tree planting efforts, and distributing tree seedlings. This is just one example; your mission should align with your unique vision. Together, your mission and vision will illuminate the purpose of your life.

Pinpoint Your Progress: The Power of Precise Goal Setting:

In the 'PERFECT' goal-setting formula, the letter 'P' stands for another word, 'PRECISE'. 'Precise' in goal setting is crucial because it defines your objectives clearly and succinctly. When you articulate your goals precisely, you can easily explain them to yourself and others in just a few words. For example, saying "I want to be a businessman" is a broad statement that lacks specificity because it doesn't clarify what kind of business or what specific role you aspire to.

By making your goals precise, you bring focus and clarity to your aspirations. This precision helps you avoid ambiguity and provides a clear direction for your efforts. When you know exactly what you want to achieve, it becomes easier to devise a plan and take actionable steps towards your goal. This focused approach increases your efficiency and effectiveness in pursuing your objectives.

Moreover, precise goals enhance motivation and commitment. When you have a clear understanding of your goal, you can better visualize the outcomes and benefits of achieving it. This clarity of purpose fuels your determination and perseverance, especially when faced with challenges or setbacks along the way.

Furthermore, precise goals facilitate better communication and collaboration with others. When you can clearly articulate your goals, you can enlist support from mentors, colleagues, or stakeholders who can help you achieve them. They will understand your vision and can provide valuable insights or resources to aid in your journey.

In summary, aiming for precision in goal setting is essential for achieving success. It transforms vague aspirations into tangible objectives, providing a roadmap for action and enabling you to stay focused, motivated, and aligned with your vision. By being precise about your goals, you set yourself up for greater clarity, efficiency, and ultimately, success in your endeavors.

'Setting a precise goal is like using a torchlight in a dark room—it helps illuminate the path ahead, guiding you towards your destination with clarity and focus.'

Embracing Eagerness: The Second Letter 'E' in the PERFECT Goal-Setting Formula

The second letter 'E' in the word 'PERFECT' highlights 'eagerness,' synonymous with interest. Without eagerness towards a goal, neither greed nor motivation can sustain your efforts. Eagerness is essential; without it, reaching your goal becomes improbable. Therefore, when setting goals, it's crucial to introspect and identify your genuine interests.

Today, many youths and families prioritize fields with abundant current opportunities. However, this often leads to higher risks of failure or depression later on. Consider this example: Recently, I spoke with one of my students who excelled in software engineering but suffered from depression. She reached out seeking relief. During our conversation, it became evident that her depression stemmed from neglecting her true interests. Initially passionate about Electronics and Telecommunication and aspiring to work in electronics production, she was dissuaded by reports of limited job prospects and inferior salary structures. Yielding to family advice and societal pressures favoring fields with apparent benefits, she pursued software engineering instead. While securing a well-paying job, her lack of enthusiasm left her feeling unfulfilled and depressed.

This case illustrates how overlooking personal interests can lead to dissatisfaction, even after achieving success. For many, a lack of eagerness proves a significant hurdle to success, as it inevitably dampens motivation. It's natural to initially pursue a goal for a brief period, only to abandon it for something else due to disinterest, resulting in heightened stress. Genuine interest in a goal acts as a magnetic force, drawing you towards it. Thus, before embarking on any goal, it's essential to assess your level of interest in and passion for it.

From Responsibility to Results: How "R" Empowers Your Goals:

The third letter of 'PERFECT' stands for two words, with 'Responsibility' being the first.

Responsibility entails taking ownership of the actions needed to achieve your goals. It's crucial not to rely excessively on others to accomplish what you've set out to do. For instance, imagine you've set a goal for health that requires daily morning exercise. Initially, waking up at 5 a.m. might be a significant challenge. You might ask a family member or friend to wake you up at that time every day. While they may help initially, they may not be able to do it consistently. If you rely on them entirely, missing their wake-up call could disrupt your routine, jeopardizing your progress towards your goal. Thus, true responsibility means ensuring you can independently meet the demands of your goals, without overly depending on external support.

Don't Wish on a Star: Setting 'Realistic' Goals for Lasting Change:

The letter 'R' stands for the second word, 'REALISTIC'. Here it is very important to understand what exactly this word wants to indicate! The person who first believed in the possibility of humans flying like birds or traveling to the moon faced a goal or idea that seemed unreal at that time. At that moment, maybe it was nothing but an impossible; pipe dream for the whole world. But do you know why it has been implemented? At least one believed with all his heart that it could be done, none but one knew it was realistic, so he made it happen. So in setting goals, you have to clearly see that this goal may seem unrealistic to the whole world as if only one word comes out from inside you 'It is realistic, it can be done'.

Fuelling Fascination: How the "F" in "PERFECT" Makes Your Work Shine:

'PERFECT' with its middle fourth letter 'F' signifies 'Fascination', which denotes a deep attraction. For instance, if you have a strong fascination for football—enjoying watching it, practicing it, and feeling eager to play whenever you see a football field—it would be challenging to develop the same level of passion and focus towards cricket if you were enrolled in a cricket training centre instead. Therefore, before setting goals in any field, it's essential to assess whether you genuinely feel fascinated by that subject. This fascination should stem from a genuine interest within you, not merely from fleeting emotions or superficial attractions driven by external factors like greed.

Going Green with PERFECT: The Essential Role of Ecology:

The fifth letter 'E' of 'PERFECT' represents Ecology, which assesses harmony. There are two types: Internal Ecology and External Ecology. Achieving any goal or desired outcome requires balancing these two ecologies. Otherwise, progress may stagnate, leading to a sense of stagnation or a lack of momentum.

Internal Ecology involves examining any internal obstacles or conflicts that may hinder your goal-setting process. It's crucial to identify and resolve these conflicts, understanding the underlying reasons behind them. This may involve addressing subconscious resistance or evaluating how the changes required by the goal align with existing habits and lifestyles. Mental readiness to embrace lifestyle changes post-goal achievement is also key.

External Ecology complements Internal Ecology by assessing external factors. It's essential to evaluate whether your environment, including family support, is conducive or obstructive to your goals. If external conditions are unfavorable, taking proactive steps to shift them in favor of your aspirations becomes necessary. This might involve communicating your goals to gain support or devising strategies to navigate and overcome external challenges.

In essence, achieving balance between Internal and External Ecology ensures alignment, fostering a conducive environment for sustained progress towards your goals.

When considering the external ecology, it's crucial to anticipate how environmental conditions may shift once you achieve your goal. These changes should align with your expectations and personal values. For instance, if your goal involves starting a business abroad that requires extended periods away from home, but you're not emotionally prepared for the separation from your family, or if your family is reluctant to support your decision to go abroad, these conflicts can create significant mental stress. Such challenges often lead to missed opportunities as the alignment between personal aspirations and external realities becomes crucial for sustainable success. If you check the external ecology while determining the outcome to take precautions in advance then you will not have to face such obstacles.

Craving Success? The Secret Ingredient in Your PERFECT Goals:

The sixth letter 'C' of 'PERFECT' indicates 'CRAVING' i.e., strong desire. No matter how much you have an interest in and attraction towards a thing, but if you don't have a strong desire to get it, you will never go searching for that thing. It's proven that only strong desire can keep motivation levels at an all-time high. Craving is a strong feeling of wanting or getting something. Your goal can pull you towards it if you have a strong craving for it. We rarely remember to drink water during the day but when we feel very thirsty we can run anywhere in search of water, do whatever we want, even dig the ground to find a source of water to quench our thirst. Similarly, if you have a strong desire, thirst for the goal, then you will forget everything else and be engaged in achieving it.

Craving is a noun derived from crave, which comes from the Old English word crafian, which literally means 'to demand'. If there is no demand we will become inactive. Because there is demand, people are growing crops today, and because there is demand, fishermen are crossing the deep sea by boat at the risk of their lives!

It has been observed that the more intense a person's craving for a goal is, the more likely they are to achieve it.

Why is it necessary to have strong craving to set any goal and achieve it?

Motivation: Desire acts as a high-level motivator. It boosts your passion and enthusiasm and activates you to take action towards your goals. When you have a deep desire for something, you go the extra mile and put in the effort and time required to achieve it.

Ambition: Hunger – thirst or craving helps you persevere in the face of obstacles and setbacks. Even after setting a goal, there are many people who, when faced with the slightest obstacle or challenge, give up taking the necessary steps to achieve the goal, or even change their goals. But 'crave' acts as a follower that reminds you again and again why you started! It keeps you focused and determined, allowing you to overcome setbacks and persevere until you reach your goals.

Positive mind-set: Having a strong desire helps you maintain a positive mind-set. This enables you to bounce back from failure or disappointment more effectively. Instead of giving up in the face of adversity, your desire encourages you to learn from your mistakes and keep going. It also encourages finding alternative routes if needed.

Energy and motivation: Craving creates a high level of energy and motivation to persevere towards your goals. Craving provides a sense of excitement to make your wishes come true. Its energy and enthusiasm can boost your productivity and creativity. Instills innovative energy in you and helps you stay committed to your goals.

However, it is worth noting that 'craving' is a powerful driving force, so it should never be ignored while setting goals. It is important to ensure that your desires are aligned with your values and purpose to ensure sustainable and meaningful goal pursuits.

Don't Get Lost in the Fog: How 'Time-Bound' Goals Keep You on Track:

The last letter of 'PERFECT', 'T', emphasizes the crucial concept of being 'Time Bound'. Our minds often procrastinate when tasks lack clarity on why they must be done and how long they will take to achieve. While understanding the 'why' is driven by purpose, knowing 'how long' is essential for effective planning and motivation.

For example, imagine aspiring to achieve financial success by becoming a billionaire. Without a clear timeframe—such as aiming to reach this milestone within five or ten years—it's challenging to devise a concrete plan. A well-informed plan is vital for navigating challenges and ensuring success. Therefore, time-bounding your goals are essential for setting realistic expectations and facilitating strategic planning towards achieving them.

Let's consider an example related to career advancement:

Imagine you're an ambitious professional aiming for a senior management position in your company. You're clear on your goal to reach this level because it aligns with your career aspirations and personal growth. However, without setting a time-bound target, such as aiming to achieve this promotion within the next three years, your path forward may lack clarity.

With a defined timeframe in mind, you can now strategize effectively. You might plan to acquire additional skills, take on more challenging projects, and build strong relationships within your industry. This clarity helps you stay focused and motivated, making it easier to track your progress and adjust your efforts as needed. By being time-bound, you set yourself up for success by turning your aspirations into achievable milestones.

Now, let's get to the point of how you should apply the 'PERFECT' formula!

There are five vital areas in our lives: health, wealth, success, love and relationships, and happiness. Life cannot be fulfilling unless we achieve success in all these areas. A true balance in life cannot exist without it. Therefore, it's crucial to set goals gradually, defining outcomes for each area. So while setting goals, focus on each of these areas one by one and envision your ideal success in each domain as the starting point.

Next, apply the 'PERFECT' goal-setting formula to ensure your dreams align with your purpose. Evaluate if your goals are precise and clearly defined, assess your eagerness to achieve them, and determine if you're ready to take full responsibility. Consider the realism of your goals and how fascinated you are by them. Check your internal and external ecology whether your feelings are congruent and how supportive your environment is. Lastly, gauge your intense cravings for these outcomes. Set a realistic timeframe to achieve each goal.

To illustrate, let's take 'health' as an example from the five areas. If your current weight exceeds healthy norms for your height and age, and your energy levels are low, but you envision a strong, energetic body at a balanced weight ratio for your age and height, that becomes your desired outcome. Apply the 'PERFECT' formula methodically to ensure your purpose, precision, eagerness, responsibility; realism, fascination, ecology and your cravings all align with your health goals. Set a specific timeframe to achieve this outcome. Adjust your goals as necessary if conflicts arise, ensuring they always align with your evolving needs and aspirations.

Assessing Your Present State: A Vital Step towards Success

Hopefully, by using the 'PERFECT' goal-setting formula, you have a clear idea of your destination, i.e., you have formed a crystal clear picture in your mind of where you want to take yourself in the next few years. Now you need to know your present state, i.e., from where you will start your journey to success. Maybe you have to start from scratch, or you have at least a little bit of resources, or you have to start from the debt! Take time and be clear to yourself exactly from where you are starting your journey, how much knowledge and skills you have, how much debt you have, and what resources do you have, or what the main problems you are facing now. Understanding your present state is pivotal when embarking on the journey to success, much akin to any other life journey. It serves as a crucial starting point that provides clarity and direction for your purpose. By knowing where you currently stand—whether starting from scratch, having limited resources, or managing debt—you gain a realistic perspective on what needs to be accomplished and the steps required to get there.

Moreover, assessing your present state allows for effective planning and resource management. It enables you to allocate resources wisely, and identify areas where improvement or additional support may be necessary. This awareness not only enhances your ability to make informed decisions but also boosts motivation by highlighting progress made and areas needing attention.

Furthermore, understanding your present circumstances helps in anticipating challenges and risks that may arise along the way. This foresight empowers you to develop contingency plans and strategies to overcome obstacles, thereby increasing your chances of sustained progress and success.

Ultimately, by acknowledging and evaluating your present state, you lay a solid foundation for personal growth and development. It promotes self-awareness, encourages continuous improvement, and fosters resilience in pursuing your aspirations. Thus, knowing your present state is not just important but essential in initiating and navigating the journey towards achieving your goals and realizing your full potential.

Crafting the Path to Triumph: Strategic Planning for Success

The second step to success is strategic planning. After you have an idea of your desire state (destination) and your present state, you need to plan to bridge the gap between the two. Here I mean planning about the way to reach the destination and the resources needed to get there. An example can make it easier, suppose you have decided to go to Medellin, a certain city in Colombia, and you are in a city around Kolkata. So first, you need to see which international airport is near Medellin and which international airport is near your city from where you can start your journey. Then you have to book a flight ticket to reach your destination at the specified time, and then you have to see what mode of transport you have to use to reach the airport from your home, maybe you have to take a bus, then a taxi, etc. You also need to know when exactly you should leave home to reach the airport at the right time, which bus route to take, how to get to your destination after landing at Jose Maria Cordova International Airport, where you will stay, how much money it will cost to complete the journey or what resources will be needed -you have to have a specific plan in advance about all those things, and only then can you complete a successful journey. In the same way, you have to make specific plans to achieve specific goals in life, otherwise you will be disoriented in the middle and will be forced to leave everything and go back to the old ways or drown in the darkness of regret.

But never think that everything you plan will be perfect or that everything will be according to your plan. Sometimes the plan may fail, it should not be wiped out because you have to understand that there may be some errors in your plan, so you have to find new ways and join the action quickly. It is not right to think that all methods will work equally well; there is a need to have flexibility so that you can change the strategy if necessary. In the life of common people or any highly successful person, everything never goes according to plan. Even the most successful people sometimes get derailed, but they are successful because they are able to get themselves back on track as quickly as possible. On the other hand, the failure or the average person, once derailed, does not take the necessary steps to get back on track or even try to get back on track, and this is where a huge difference develops between the average person and the extremely successful person.

How to plan strategically to a large extent?

Break the path from your current state to your destination into small, time-proportioned chunks. In order to explain more clearly, it is necessary to give an example; suppose you want to own 100 crore rupees in the next 10 years i.e.,, here your outcome is to earn 100 crore rupees and you have maybe 9 years, 11 months, and 29 days. Assuming your current income is zero, i.e.,, this is your present state. From this position, you may naturally think that the target of 100 crore is a huge target level, and even sometimes you may doubt yourself whether it is actually possible to achieve it! But this 100 crore earning target will seem easy or attainable to you if you break it into smaller chunks, we can call them milestones. For example, if you decide that you will earn 5 lakh rupees in the next year, then this is your first milestone. If you want, you can divide it into smaller parts and set monthly or quarterly targets. Now, see what you need to do to cross your first milestone; maybe you need to start a business, maybe you need more knowledge or something else; however, plan for them separately.

Perfect planning begins with a deliberate process: sit down with a pen and notepad, and engage your mind by asking specific questions. For instance, pose the question, "What do I need to do to earn five lakh rupees in a year?" Your mind will generate multiple responses; jot them down immediately. Then, continue asking, "What else could be done in other ways?" This iterative questioning will unveil new possibilities—write them all down.

After several rounds of inquiry, review the collected answers. Filter through them and select those that align best with your goals and purpose. For each selected idea, strategize meticulously. This method ensures thorough exploration of options and empowers you to craft a comprehensive plan tailored to your aspirations and circumstances.

In essence, effective planning involves proactive engagement with your thoughts, methodically exploring various avenues, and selecting the most promising strategies to propel you towards success.

Once you understand your first milestone, you need to plan your day accordingly. When strategizing, clarity emerges on which tasks hold the utmost urgency and importance for you. These tasks should take precedence and be placed in the top tier of your priorities. Simultaneously, identify those tasks that are important but less urgent, and organize them accordingly. Make a list of tasks that are less important, which you may delegate or eliminate as appropriate. This method of prioritization, as previously mentioned in our discussion on creating a daily schedule, simplifies adherence to your plan. Aligning your daily schedule with your action plan is integral to executing it effectively. Use time blocking to allocate specific periods for different tasks, maintaining focus and reducing distractions. Establish a consistent daily routine to foster discipline and reinforce productive habits, while allowing flexibility to adapt to unforeseen changes. End each day with a reflection on the progress made, assessing what worked well and what can be improved, and use these insights to adjust your plans for the following days.

Additionally, it is crucial to assess whether you possess the necessary resources to achieve your goals, such as manpower, financial capital, or required knowledge and skills for business ventures. If these resources are lacking, it becomes imperative to devise a specific strategy outlining how and from where you will acquire them. Only through this proactive approach can your strategic plan be thoroughly perfected to align with your overarching objectives.

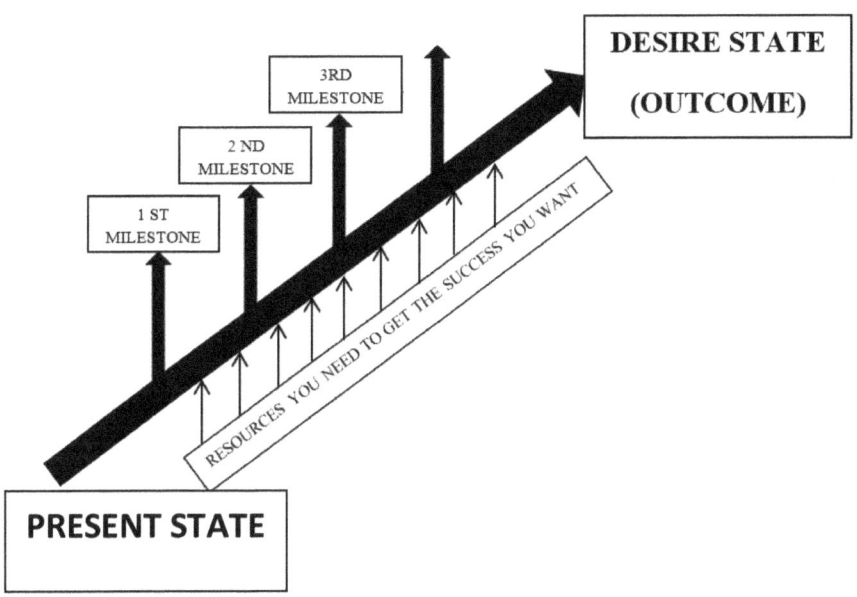

After achieving your first milestone, the journey to continued success involves setting new milestones and devising specific action plans to achieve them in a timely manner. This process begins with evaluating your progress, reflecting on what strategies were effective and identifying areas for improvement. Defining the next milestone clearly is crucial, this ensures that each new target aligns with your long-term goals and provides a clear path forward.

The Momentum of Action: Mastering the Push-Pull Method for Achieving Success

"Action produces results"

After setting a goal and making a specific plan to achieve it, the next most important step is to take action on the plan consistently and regularly to achieve that goal. If you are not enthusiastic about work, then refrain from taking action; otherwise, you may find yourself daydreaming without hope of results. To achieve or change results, action must be taken, sometimes on a large scale as needed.

Usually, people set goals and plan to achieve them, but in most cases, the reason for failure is the lack of continuous action in that direction. Taking proper action is the cornerstone of achieving results and creating success. Regardless of how clear and compelling our goals are, it is the actions we take toward these goals that ultimately determine our outcomes.

Why is it so important to take the actions to achieve success?

Transforming Vision into Reality:

Proper action is the bridge between a vision and its realization. While a goal sets the destination, actions are the steps taken to reach there. Each step brings one closer to the end result, gradually transforming the abstract vision into tangible reality.

Transforming ideas into reality:

Only ideas have no real value unless they are implemented. Taking action helps you implement your ideas by testing them in the real world and testing their suitability and effectiveness.

Overcome fear and resistance:

Often, fear and resistance can prevent us from pursuing our goals. By taking action we confront and overcome these obstacles, building resilience and confidence along the way.

Learning through experience:

Actions provide opportunities for learning and growth. Action transforms your knowledge into skills making it much more valuable. Experience gained by taking action is a powerful teacher that helps you refine your techniques and improve your chances of success.

Building momentum:

Taking action creates momentum, and sustaining it leads to progress. You know very well how much trouble we have to set a stationary object in motion, but how easy it is to move it once it is set in motion. Such continuous action not only speeds up our work but also makes our work much easier.

Each step builds upon the other and moves you closer to your goal. Action instills motivation and enthusiasm, making it easier to sustain your efforts and persevere in the face of challenges.

Creating Discipline:

Behind every great success lies discipline. Taking action consistently creates discipline. In today's age where electronic gadgets and social media dominate, it is normal to lose focus, mind clutter is more likely. But taking consistent action will help you focus and avoid distractions.

Overcoming the Paralysis of Overthinking or Analyzing:'

Overthinking and overanalyzing can lead to a state of paralysis, halting progress. Taking action helps break free from this cycle and propels you towards success. It teaches you to learn from real-world experience instead of getting bogged down in theoretical thinking.

Pusher and puller to speed up the action

A moving object also becomes motionless if no force is applied to it, i.e.,, it is not pulled or pushed. If we want to increase the speed of any object, we have to apply the force on it and at the same time we have to increase the level of force. We have seen that when a force is applied to an object, there are usually two forces, one for pushing and one for pulling, and in cases where both forces are applied, there is almost no chance of deceleration. In the same way to accelerate our progress, to increase its rate, we must find pusher and puller in the same direction.

Now the question is "who or what is there from outside that will constantly pull or push us? Who or what is there to keep you motivated all the time, pushing or pulling you to speed up the process of success?" Rest assured that this job is probably difficult to get along with someone! So what can be done?

Yes, it doesn't take anything but to appreciate and enjoy the power of inspiration from within that pulls and pushes you well. You can significantly enhance your path to success by harnessing the natural inclination of your mind to avoid pain as motivation and the desire for pleasure as inspiration.

Visualization can be a potent technique to harness intrinsic motivation by leveraging our natural tendency to avoid pain.

Here's how you can effectively utilize visualization for this purpose:

Visualization Technique for Intrinsic Motivation through Pain Avoidance (THE PUSHER)

1. Create a Detailed Mental Image

Begin by finding a quiet and comfortable space where you can focus without distractions. Close your eyes and vividly imagine the consequences of not taking action towards your goal. Visualize the potential negative outcomes and pain points associated with remaining stagnant or not pursuing your aspirations.

2. Engage Your Senses

As you visualize, engage multiple senses to make the scenario as real and impactful as possible. Imagine how it would feel emotionally—such as regret, frustration, or disappointment. Visualize the physical consequences or limitations that might arise from not achieving your goal.

3. Heighten Emotional Connection

Allow yourself to deeply connect with the emotions that arise during this visualization. Feel the discomfort or unease associated with the potential negative outcomes. Emotions can serve as powerful motivators, compelling you to take action to avoid these undesirable consequences.

4. Immerse Yourself in Future Scenarios

Project yourself into the future where you haven't pursued your goal. Visualize the day-to-day implications of not achieving what you desire. See how it impacts various aspects of your life—personal satisfaction, relationships, career, or health.

5. Maintain Focus and Commitment

Use the emotions and insights gained from your visualization to maintain focus and commitment to your goals. Keep the mental image of potential pain points as a reminder of why you need to take action and stay dedicated to your journey.

6. Repeat Two or Three Times

Do this visualization technique two or three more times if necessary to reinforce your intrinsic motivation. Each session allows you to deepen your emotional connection with the pain of inaction and.

7. Take Action

Finally, translate your motivation into action, consistent actions towards your goals to prevent the potential pain you visualized and move closer to realizing your aspirations.

Visualization harnesses the power of our mind's tendency to avoid pain by immersing ourselves in the consequences of inaction. By vividly imagining the negative outcomes of not pursuing our goals, we can cultivate intrinsic motivation to take proactive steps towards success. Use this technique to strengthen your resolve, maintain focus, and propel yourself forward on your journey of personal growth and achievement.

THE PULLER WITHIN

Our innate desire to seek pleasure serves as a potent motivator that propels us towards our goals. When we experience pleasure, our brain releases dopamine, a neurotransmitter linked with feelings of reward and satisfaction. This release initiates a positive reinforcement loop, driving us to seek out behaviors and actions that lead to pleasurable experiences.

Pleasure often arises from activities that resonate with our interests, emotions, and values. When we engage in these pursuits and find joy or fulfilment, it strengthens our motivation to persist in our endeavours. This intrinsic motivation stems from the inherent satisfaction we derive from aligning our actions with what brings us happiness and fulfilment.

As we continue to pursue goals that bring us pleasure, whether through personal interests, meaningful relationships, or achievements aligned with our values, we reinforce our commitment and drive. The cycle of dopamine release in response to these pleasurable experiences further fuels our motivation, creating a dynamic where the pursuit of our goals becomes not only purposeful but also deeply satisfying.

Understanding and leveraging the power of pleasure in motivating ourselves underscores the importance of aligning our actions with our genuine passions and values. By cultivating experiences that bring us joy and satisfaction along our journey, we foster enduring motivation and a sense of fulfilment in pursuing our aspirations.

Visualization Technique: Harnessing Pleasure as Motivation

Visualization can be a powerful tool to harness the motivation derived from pleasure. By vividly imagining pleasurable experiences associated with achieving your goals, you can strengthen your intrinsic drive and commitment. Here's how to effectively use visualization for this purpose:

1. Create a Relaxing Environment

Find a quiet and comfortable space where you won't be disturbed. Sit or lie down in a relaxed position, close your eyes, and take a few deep breaths to calm your mind and body.

2. Visualize Your Desired Goal

Begin by visualizing your goal as if it has already been achieved. Imagine yourself in the future, experiencing the outcome you desire. Visualize the specific details: where you are, who you are with, and how you feel in that moment of accomplishment.

3. Engage Your Senses

Immerse yourself in the visualization by engaging all your senses. See the surroundings vividly, hear the sounds associated with success, and feel the emotions of joy, satisfaction, and fulfilments. Make the experience as real and sensory-rich as possible.

4. Connect with Emotional Responses

Focus on the emotions that arise during the visualization. Feel the happiness, pride, and fulfilments that come with achieving your goal. Allow these positive emotions to intensify as you continue to visualize the scene.

5. Anchor the Experience

Create a mental anchor to reinforce the positive emotions associated with your goal achievement. This could be a word, phrase, or image that encapsulates the feelings of pleasure and satisfaction you experience in your visualization.

6. Revisit Regularly

Practice this visualization technique regularly, ideally daily. Each session allows you to reinforce your connection with the pleasurable outcomes of achieving your goals. As you consistently visualize success, you strengthen your motivation and commitment to taking action.

7. Use Visualization as Motivational Fuel

Use the positive emotions and motivation generated from your visualization sessions to fuel your actions towards your goals. Let the anticipation of experiencing pleasure and fulfilments drive your determination and perseverance.

8. Take Inspired Action

Translate your motivation into concrete action steps. Use the energy and clarity gained from your visualization exercises to set day schedule, create plans for, and take consistent steps towards achieving them. Act with confidence, knowing that you are moving closer to the pleasurable experiences you've visualized.

9. Celebrate Progress

Celebrate small victories along the way. Acknowledge and appreciate each step you take towards your goal. Celebrating progress reinforces your motivation and reinforces the positive association between action and pleasure.

10. Reflect and Adjust

Regularly reflect on your visualization experiences and the progress you've made. Evaluate whether your goals and actions are still aligned with your values and aspirations. Adjust your visualization exercises and action plans as needed to maintain focus and momentum.

Outcome: Discovering Solutions and Making Decisions

In our daily lives, we encounter a multitude of experiences that shape our emotional and mental states. Many of these moments bring us joy and uplift our spirits, fostering a sense of resourcefulness within us. Conversely, there are instances that lead us into states of mind where we feel less capable or burdened.

Every day presents its own set of challenges. Some are easily resolved, while others leave us perplexed, unsure of the best course of action. When faced with seemingly insurmountable problems, our emotions such as sadness, worry, fear, and anxiety naturally intensify. In such times, our mental state becomes less resourceful, hindering our ability to make sound decisions.

To illustrate this effectively, let's consider that you're currently grappling with a significant challenge in your life. It could be financial difficulties, a breakup in a relationship or love life, concerns about your children's education or future, overwhelming work or family pressures, or any other pressing issue.

Despite your best efforts—thinking creatively, applying various strategies, and exerting considerable effort—you may find yourself at an impasse. It might even seem that this problem has no solution, or that it's insurmountable and you'll never find relief from it. In such circumstances, it's natural to hesitate in making decisions, especially since psychology emphasizes that important and accurate decisions are difficult to make in an unresourceful state of mind. So, what steps can one take?

Should one rely on others to solve the problem or make decisions? Alternatively, is there a way to empower oneself to tackle the issue independently and make informed, accurate decisions?

Consider how fish obtain oxygen to survive! Just as we humans breathe in oxygen directly from the air, fish have a fascinating adaptation: they absorb dissolved oxygen from water. Fish accomplish this by drawing water into their mouths (through a nostril-like opening just above the mouth). Inside their bodies, they have specialized organs called gills which extract oxygen from the water and release it into their bloodstream. The water devoid of oxygen is then expelled.

Remarkably, fish can perform this essential process effortlessly, regardless of how deep they are in the water.

Have you ever noticed what the fish do when the oxygen content of the water is reduced for some reason especially when the water level is reduced or the water gets polluted? Those who know or have seen this are aware that the fish then rises to the surface of the water and tries to take oxygen directly from the air. In fact, when fish realize that they are no longer getting the oxygen they need for their bodies from the water, they try to solve their problems by leaving their most comfortable position, their known suitable environment for survival. Fish also realize that the problem is actually in the water, so they separate (disassociate) their mouths from the water to take oxygen directly from the air and solve the problem.

Similarly in our lives, finding solutions to problems and making sound decisions often requires stepping out of the current environment or state of mind in which the problem originated. It's unrealistic to expect that staying in the same place or mental state will lead to resolution or clarity. To effectively tackle a problem or make an important decision, one must explore solutions beyond the circumstances where the issue arose. It certainly does not mean that your financial problems are going on and you have left your home and family and taken refuge in the Himalayan peaks and everything is resolved or it is the right decision in life.

For instance, imagine the same problem that you faced now confronts your friend. He turns to you for guidance or depends on your decision-making. In such a scenario, and even if someone else seeks your counsel, you can draw upon various perspectives and solutions. You can provide them with thoughtful guidance, directing them towards accurate and important decisions. Not only your friend, if someone else comes to you with a problem and wants to know its solution or expect to make a decision for him, you can easily guide him. But you find yourself unable to solve a problem or hesitant to make important decisions in your own case, it's often because you're deeply immersed in the situation. Your personal involvement can cloud your judgment and make it difficult to see a clear path forward.

However, when it comes to helping a friend or someone else with the same issue, you assume the role of an observer. In this disassociate position; you have the advantage of viewing the situation from an outsider's perspective. This impartial viewpoint allows you to assess the problem objectively and consider all possible aspects thoroughly. As an observer, you can more easily identify the best possible solutions and make informed decisions, leveraging your clarity and detachment to guide others effectively.

In sports like football, cricket, or any other, the coach plays a crucial role. The coach doesn't necessarily have to be the best player themselves, but they excel as observers. This role allows them to pinpoint mistakes, offer valuable advice, and guide players effectively. The coach observes everything of the players during the game or practice. I do the same thing in my Mental Wellness Mastery program, being a good observer I find solutions to people's problems very easily. You can certainly take such help from me if you feel the need, but I would say that you can become the best observer of your life and you can easily find the solution to the problem and take the right decision. How? Let's see how to do it.

If you're open to trying a mental technique, begin by setting up two chairs facing each other. Sit comfortably in one chair, either with your eyes closed or open as you prefer. Imagine another version of yourself sitting in the chair opposite you. This second version of you is facing a specific problem—something that is currently happening in your life—and is seeking your help to solve it.

Take time to observe this second version of yourself closely. Notice his situation, his mental and physical state, and his actions in response to the problem. Pay attention to his emotions, mannerisms, actions and the significance of the issue in his life. By observing as an outsider, you detach yourself from the emotional entanglement of the situation.

Once you've thoroughly observed and understood the situation, step into the role of an advisor. Offer guidance and find solutions for the version of yourself sitting before you with his life's challenge. You'll be surprised at how effortlessly various solutions come to mind.

This technique may take about twenty to thirty minutes to practice, but it can unveil multiple solutions to significant life problems—solutions that may have eluded you for months or years, causing frustration.

Moreover, this method can also aid you in making accurate and important decisions. As an observer of your own situation, you gain a comprehensive view of all aspects involved. This clarity allows you to discern the best course of action more effectively than seeking advice from others, who may understand your situation but lack the personal depth of feeling and observation you bring to it.

In essence, by becoming your own observer through this technique, you empower yourself to fully grasp the complexity of your challenges and make informed, thoughtful decisions or find creative solutions.

Conclusion

In 'Demolish Your Obstacle; Transform Your Adversities into Massive Success,' I have explored a transformative journey of overcoming challenges and turning setbacks into stepping stones towards achieving remarkable success. This book serves as a guide to harnessing the power within adversity and leveraging it to propel oneself forward.

Throughout this book, I've delved into practical strategies and profound insights on how to approach obstacles not as barriers, but as opportunities for growth and strong mind-set. By reframing adversity as a catalyst for personal and professional development, we empower ourselves to embrace challenges with courage and determination.

Key themes explored include:

Understanding Misconceptions: When faced with problems and adversity, people often feel overwhelmed and helpless. This can lead to a cycle of uncertainty, mental and physical exhaustion, and impaired judgment, making it difficult to think clearly and act decisively.

Mental Barriers and Solutions: Every problem has a solution, but overcoming mental barriers is crucial to finding it. Just as the boy in the pole-vault story succeeded by envisioning his success, you must mentally overcome obstacles to achieve tangible results.

Unlimited Power Within: The human mind holds immense power that can guide individuals through difficult times and lead to success, yet many fail to harness this potential.

The Role of the Mind: The mind acts as powerful software that manages the brain, making a significant difference in people's lives based on how well they understand and use it.

Mind vs. Brain: Despite having powerful brains, many people lack awareness and knowledge about the mind, leading to underutilization of their full potential.

Mind-set Mastery: The importance of cultivating a strong mind-set that sees adversity as a natural part of the journey towards success. By adopting a growth mind-set, we learn to extract valuable lessons from setbacks and use them to fuel our progress.

Strategic Action: Strategies for taking proactive steps in the face of adversity, from setting clear goals and creating actionable plans to maintaining focus and perseverance. These strategies help navigate through obstacles and stay committed to achieving long-term objectives.

Embracing Change: This book will teach you to embrace change as a constant and inevitable aspect of personal and professional growth. Adapting to challenges and using them as opportunities for innovation and improvement are important skills discussed in the book.

Transformative Success Stories: Inspirational stories and real-life examples of individuals who have overcome significant challenges to achieve extraordinary success. These stories serve as motivational examples of how mind-set, determination, and strategic thinking can lead to breakthroughs.

Unveiling the Steps to Success: Success, often perceived as an elusive destination, becomes attainable when we embrace a structured approach. Our roadmap begins with clarity of purpose—setting clear, meaningful goals that ignite our passion and drive. Each goal acts as a guiding star, illuminating our path through uncertainty and adversity.

Decision Making and Solution: Significant life challenges often leave us feeling stuck, prompting a need for detachment to gain clarity. Adopting an observer's perspective can facilitate deeper insight and more effective problem-solving. Practicing the mental technique of visualizing oneself as an advisor can lead to innovative solutions and informed decisions, enhancing personal empowerment and growth.

As I conclude my journey through 'Demolish Your Obstacle; Transform Your Adversities into Massive Success,' remember that adversity is not a roadblock but a path to greatness. By integrating the principles and strategies outlined in this book, you are equipped to turn every obstacle into a stepping stone towards your own version of massive success.

Embrace challenges with resilience, maintain unwavering determination, and harness the power within adversity to propel yourself towards achieving your dreams. Let this book be your guide and companion on the journey to demolishing obstacles and transforming adversity into lasting success.

The path ahead is yours to forge. With the right mind-set, strategic action, and a commitment to continuous growth, you have the potential to achieve greatness beyond measure. Start today, embrace your journey, and witness the transformative power of overcoming adversity on your path to massive success.

A garden is a sanctuary of beauty, growth, and transformation. Every plant, every flower, every tree in the garden has its own unique journey, beauty, and importance. Our lives are like a magnificent flower garden, filled with beauty, fragrance, and charm. This allure draws many people in, who enter and delight in its splendour. In our garden of life, some people come to love, some to care, and many to enjoy the joy of plucking its beautiful flowers. Others may leave footprints with thorned shoes, causing pain and disturbance. Every moment and every person who enters our life holds value and importance. Some situations or individuals may wound us, leaving scars that take time to heal. However, there are also countless beautiful people and moments that bring happiness and prosperity, enriching our lives in ways that make the journey worthwhile. Yet, in the careful arrangement of this beautiful garden lies the essence of our happiness and the fullness of life.

When new flowers bloom, symbolizing new achievements and adding color to our lives, it reflects the true meaning of our human existence. The success, happiness, and fulfilment of your life are hidden within this well-tended garden.

Therefore, nurture this garden of your life with care and devotion, regardless of who may trample it or who may seek to destroy its beauty. It is within this garden that you will find the profound success, happiness, and fulfilment that define your life's journey.

Share the gift of transformation with your loved ones by giving them this life-changing book, empowering them to overcome obstacles just as you have.

www.ingramcontent.com/pod-product-compliance
Lightning Source LLC
LaVergne TN
LVHW061549070526
838199LV00077B/6964